WORKSHOP/APD HOMES

ARCHITECTURE, INTERIORS, AND THE SPACES BETWEEN

WORKSHOP/APD HOMES
ARCHITECTURE, INTERIORS, AND THE SPACES BETWEEN

ANDREW KOTCHEN   MATT BERMAN

WRITTEN WITH MARC KRISTAL

RIZZOLI
NEW YORK

New York Paris London Milan

TABLE OF CONTENTS

INTRODUCTION

THE SPACES BETWEEN

Let us begin with a pertinent question: How important is the particular dynamic of a partnership to the success of an architecture/design office?

It depends. At some firms, principals with a shared sensibility collaborate closely on everything that crosses the drafting table. Elsewhere, the work might be divided up based on each of the partners' strengths or weaknesses, i.e., you take the residences, I'll handle the institutions. There are offices in which one person pursues clients, another deals with traffic management, and someone else does the designing. Still others are dominated by a signature-style celebrity, whose associates essentially serve as ghost creators.

These examples, you will have noticed, focus on the "professional." At Workshop/APD, however, the crucial dynamic between us— Andrew Kotchen and Matthew Berman, the firm's founding principals—is deeply personal. Who we are, and how we relate to each other as people, lies at the heart of our portfolio.

And it's paradoxical. In certain, indeed perhaps most respects, it would not be too much to say that we are interchangeable: two guys who grew up in Connecticut and went to the same architecture school (where we pledged the same fraternity), both family men, intensely focused professionally and demanding of ourselves and each another. Yet it is not our myriad similarities but the small, significant space between us that brings what we do to life.

Simply put, Andrew focuses on "what is," and Matt's the one who asks "what if?" For Andrew, each of the firm's projects belongs to a continuum, and springs from a consistent philosophy of practice that has only grown stronger, and more lucid, with experience and time. Accordingly, Andrew arrives at a project's governing conceit rapidly, and pursues it with a swift surety that nonetheless leaves room for innovation. Matt, conversely, begins every new project by posing new questions, releasing his natural curiosity to rethink, re-invent, and reevaluate what Workshop/APD has done in the past, and ponder how *this time*, creativity's trajectory might go differently.

Yet if these differences seem like an invitation to stasis, the re-ality is in fact precisely the opposite. In practice, it is Andrew's instinct to stick to the creative highway and remain focused on a project's final destination that gives Matt the confidence to pull off at every exit and do some exploring. And it is the ideas and inspirations that Matt retrieves on his diversions that enrich the road on which Andrew so doggedly drives. Of course—and this is the beauty of an enduring, mutually supportive partnership—sometimes we switch roles: it's Andrew who's the trapeze artist (if we may change metaphors) and Matt who serves as the safety net. The key is that someone's always flying, and someone's al-ways supporting, and that enables each of us to do our very best work—indeed, to transcend ourselves.

Therein lies the value of the space between, a gap that's translated into an exceptionally fruitful and agreeable quarter-century-long collaboration, one that has produced hundreds of completed projects of every kind, embracing architecture, and product and interior design. In the aesthetic demilitarized zone between us, the vapors of our contrasting viewpoints commingle and alchemize into something new, original, and larger than us both. If we were two guys who agreed on everything, who ratified each other's every impulse, Workshop/APD wouldn't have lasted a year. It is the space between—and the need to bridge it—that has defined our methodology of practice; the work the firm has produced; and, indeed, our endurance.

Let us add that this is a condition we enjoy and embrace. In the pages that follow, you will find projects that differ noticeably from one another—one might say that our diversity is our consis-tency. The common thread is the tension between a thing and its opposite, and how that tension is resolved. Indeed, much of our work derives its character and texture from creating harmony out of contrasting or contradictory conditions. Each project provokes a conversation about where to draw the line—one that invariably sees the line blurring, as conundrums give way to joy, to excite-ment about potential and possibility.

It is our experience, in fact, that the best architectural spaces arise from a condition of healthy tension, a tension that itself arises from an acceptance, indeed an embrace, of risk. Playing it safe, with an architectural program, a client, with oneself, means that you never leave your comfort zone, that your assumptions go unchallenged, that your work never evolves—and that everyone always approves of what you've done. Conversely, when you're willing to sail off into the unknown—when you're prepared to ask questions instead of providing ready answers—you can begin to explore the uncharted, the perplexing, and the sublime. And that has, in large measure, remained the source of our strength.

Our partnership has certainly generated a fair share of healthy tension. But the experience of entering, over and again, the spaces between has for the both of us been exhilarating and rewarding, and helped us to create a practice that we approach, every day, with enthusiasm, gratitude, and—not least—mutual respect. What follows is a record of the journey to date, and the intriguing route by which we went from Then to Now. We hope that you'll find this long, strange trip as interesting, illuminating, and enjoyable as it has been for us.

A STATE OF BECOMING

You will not be surprised to learn that the dynamic produced by the space between us, as designers and individuals, morphed at the very start of our practice into an involvement—call it an obsession—with the space *between* spaces.

From Workshop/APD's beginning, more than twenty years ago, we were fortunate enough to have loyal and trusting clients—we had work. But hungry as we were, it seemed important to make time to think, abstractly and critically, about where the values and opportunities lay in any given project. Perhaps it had to do with the fact that we'd yet to fully "arrive" in a professional sense, but for whatever reason, we began to view the very idea of "arrival" as ambiguous, a condition of stasis.

As we were just out of grad school, not into accepting the givens, very into challenging assumptions, we began to apply this philosophy to received notions about rooms. Of course we lavished much time and attention on the ones we designed. And yet, having arrived in a room, we reasoned, you become static, you're *there*. What about the process of *getting* there: did not the transition spaces—the active zones—offer their own creative (and typically overlooked) opportunities?

Matt had always been attracted to the idea of the gerund, the verb that's also a noun and describes an action that's neither started nor ended but, rather, remains in process. Accordingly, instead of thinking about boxes—bedroom, living room, bath, study—we began to consider sleeping, entertaining, bathing, studying, and how these and other gerunds might, not only break down the barriers between the boxes but become the architecture itself. What, after all, is architecture if not bodies in space? Subtract the bodies, and all you've got is sculpture. Thus we began to question how the movement of bodies through space might inform how the space would actually look.

In the early stages of a project's development, architects will often create something called a bubble diagram as a way to roughly apportion space. It's simple and effective: on a piece of tracing paper, you draw a series of blobs—bubbles—to approximate the size, shape, location, and adjacencies of the zones within a particular plan. We kept the basic idea, but instead of rooms, we bubble-diagrammed gerunds: here's where you're cooking, here's where you're reading, and so forth, adjusting the square footage and location for each activity—and, critically, the ways in which people moved from one to the next—until the plan felt natural and organic: not in terms of stasis but of patterns of use.

It was of course a theoretical exercise, and we carried it to extremes, diagramming everything every which way, and creating multicolored flow lines that eventually resembled a central nervous system. But teaching ourselves to convert program—that is, rooms within a floor plan—from space into action delivered a breakthrough, our eureka moment as architectural designers: it liberated us from thinking that we had to give our clients correct, conventional solutions, and demonstrated that we could convert people's deepest desires into uniquely responsive, and entirely personal, environments.

As we began to work, our thinking about the spaces between and how they could be activated coalesced around the idea of *hybrid use*. Perhaps inevitably, circulation spines became the repositories of many of our creative experiments. One of the earliest, and richest, was a hall that could be transformed into either a powder room or a full bath, depending on the circumstances. To activate another, quite long hallway that cut through the middle of two combined apartments, we transformed it into a library with sliding bookcases, its translucent "walls" formed by screens laser-cut with images drawn from an aerial map of New York City; the dematerialized, fluid zone enabled the combining, or closing off, of different parts of the residence *(p. 298)*.

Let us quickly add that these multifunctional zones weren't about novelty, or trying to show off how clever we were. By bleeding rooms into one another, transforming the walls that demarcated one from the next into moments of activity, we were able to create homes that embraced their surroundings while opening up interior vistas; maximized the value (in every sense) of the square footage by eliminating dead zones and layering functions; and transformed the traditional fixed, predetermined floor plan into a fluid, changeable event. Though our earliest work predated the ubiquity of the Internet, you might say that we looked at homes and apartments as though they were websites: destinations that could be navigated in a multiplicity of ways, depending upon one's needs, desires, or mood.

Interestingly, approaching design from the perspective of fluidity also helps us to animate those structural components that have to remain fixed. Stairs, for example: rather than treating them as quotidian vertical transportation, they become opportunities for entrances or exits, for ever-changing perspectives, and for experiencing the materiality of surfaces in ways at once intimate, tactile, and elegant.

When you're a young firm (or, for that matter, a well-established one), it's natural to think of any time not spent hustling as time squandered. But looking back, we're very glad to have used the spaces between jobs for visioning. We embraced the time to develop a methodology of practice—to transform ourselves into a holistic architecture and design studio.

This 6,000-square-foot ensemble represents the culmination of the firm's quarter century of work on Nantucket. Asked to create a residential compound on a property without a water view, we responded by looking inward: shaping a courtyard home in which the structures communicate with one another across a multilayered outdoor room for sunbathing, swimming, and enjoying the pleasures of the garden. A long drive, terminating in a discreet entry pavilion, establishes a sense of anticipation upon arrival.

With its dark wood, linear window trim, and consistent datum line separating the walls from the cathedral ceiling, the entry pavilion, which combines the mudroom, powder bath, and laundry, establishes the home's interior aesthetic. The glazed foyer—which seems to disappear into the landscape—forms the minimalist bridge connecting to the main circulation spines.

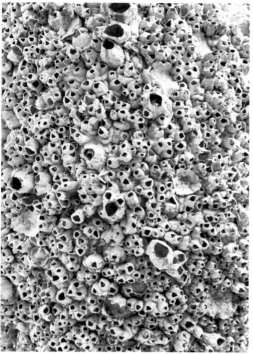

ABOVE: The figured stone in the powder room recalls the tide pools and eddies along the shoreline, an aquatic motif carried into the barnacle-covered sculptures in the transition zone. **OPPOSITE:** Leaving the entry pavilion and stepping into the glazed foyer, one encounters an axial view extending past the living/dining area to the photograph that signals the portal to the primary suite. The opening just past the floor-to-ceiling window at right leads to the children's wing.

The house's great room is loosely divided into three zones: the kitchen (with a banquette-style sofa and Roxane Lahidji salt tables abutting the island); an expansive dining table (beneath Trueing chandeliers); and the living area. Floor-to-ceiling glass sliding doors, measuring a total of forty feet in width, open nearly the entirety of the space to the lush, layered gardens in the courtyard and, beyond it, the guest quarters.

The material language of the kitchen—dark wood and gray stone—repeats in the living area fireplace, creating balance and symmetry. Similarly, the enclosed kitchen wall gives way to open decorative shelving. Simple, stylish, and casual furnishings include Workshop/APD's custom sofa, Caste's Elso coffee table, and a Ceccotti chair. A porcelain installation by Fenella Elms hangs above the fireplace.

At the end of the long main axis, just past the great room, a 90-degree turn leads to the primary suite vestibule **(OPPOSITE)**, with its view of the sitting area at the foot of the bed **(ABOVE)**. Throughout, large glazed sliding doors reflect the more contemporary architectural language of the house's interior, courtyard-facing side, while more traditional awning windows, such as the one above the bedside night table, prevail on the exterior.

As we took pains to nestle the residence into the landscape, the hallway leading past the two children's bedrooms to the media room represents an elevation change of roughly six feet from top to bottom. The doors to the kids' rooms can be glimpsed at left, on the middle level. **ABOVE:** Each child's space reflects different interests and decorative sensibilities; both look out onto the courtyard. The "geometric" wallpaper, at left, was custom designed for the setting.

The media room sits at the site's lowest level and opens directly onto the pool and its sun deck. To subtly interweave indoor and outdoor zones—and encourage fluent communication via large sliding glass doors between them— the rug's rectilinear pattern replicates the garden's geometries. The Harbour coffee table is from Workshop/APD's Signature collection.

ABOVE and RIGHT: Like the house's other components, the large, well-appointed office —a freestanding volume situated just past the media room—enjoys a soaring gabled ceiling and abundant garden-side glazing. **OPPOSITE:** This image—with its alternating solids and voids, interweaving classic architecture and landscape, and the rhythmic repetition of pure vernacular forms vitalized by a slight asymmetry—precisely encapsulates the project's intentions and spirit.

The courtyard invites habitation and facilitates easy communication between the residence's volumes while preserving their privacy and autonomy. Though the pool—in effect a "water box"—is at the garden level, i.e., the site's bottom, we set it above ground to connect it with the deck, which sits at a slightly higher elevation.

CENTRAL PARK DUPLEX

In this 5,100-square-foot duplex, in a prewar building on Manhattan's Central Park West, we were tasked with maximizing creative innovation without sacrificing the comfort and ease of a family residence. **RIGHT and BELOW LEFT:** A piquant Christopher Wool painting establishes the design's adventurous tone in the entry, lightly separated from the living/dining room by a panel of wave-patterned glass. Dmitriy & Co. created the Bandra ottoman. The "peephole" set into the wall to the left of the living room reveals a miniature landscape by Patrick Jacobs, capturing the view from the family's home in Aspen, Colorado **(BELOW RIGHT)**.

OPPOSITE and ABOVE LEFT: A hallway off the main floor's circulation spine offers a view of a digital installation we developed for the space above the stair: floating panels edged with ever-changing LED displays, à la Jenny Holzer (made more vividly present by the highly reflective walls, ceiling, and floors). **ABOVE and LEFT:** In the backlit onyx-clad box on the right-hand side of the hallway, we inserted a powder room with computer-carved striated aluminum walls, suggestive of tree bark, and a ceiling comprised of a digital display programmed to show a multitude of messages and images.

Further blurring the space between architecture and nature, a Lucio Fontana–inspired gap in the ceiling above the dining table reveals an installation of freeze-dried moss, from which we suspended a singular chandelier by Studio Drift: an armature dotted with preserved dandelion heads, each lit by an LED bulb. The skeletal form of Tom Faulkner's dining chairs enlivens the setting.

OPPOSITE, ABOVE, and RIGHT: Whimsical gold leaf "dandelion" inlays in the Workshop/APD-designed dining table might have fallen from the chandelier. Believing that ceilings typically are non-participants in the architectural experience, we "peeled" this one at the edges to create a subtle vitalization. The dining area's bar incorporates the same wavy Lasvit glass as the panel at the room's entrance. **FOLLOWING PAGES:** A large Hiroshi Sugimoto seascape, suspended above the custom elongated banquette, leavens the living room's energy. Studio Van den Akker chairs, a liquid metal Privatiselectionem table, and a custom Steinway piano complete the room.

RIGHT and BELOW: In the kitchen, the lightly veined stone enveloping the island found its way onto the countertops, backsplash, and cabinetry. Gently rolled custom brass hardware, evocative of Antoni Gaudí, welcomes the hand.

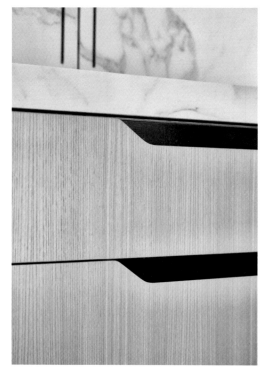

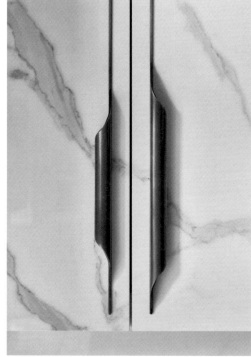

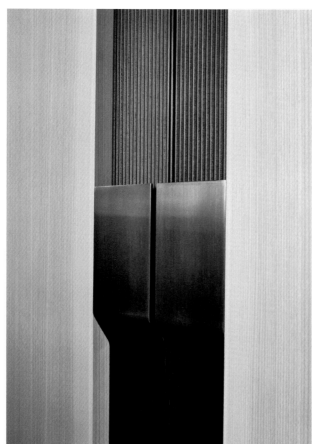

LEFT: The kitchen shares space with the family room, featuring classic designs by Frank Gehry and Pierre Paulin, as well as ultra-comfortable sofas and a Workshop/APD Signature Harbour table. *Information Wanted*, by Bethany Collins, hangs above the custom-designed sofa. **ABOVE:** A sliding bookcase with custom-crafted bronze pulls separates the family room from the home office.

The apartment's "upside-down" plan sites the bedrooms on the lower level. The primary suite is visible from the foot of the custom-designed stair (above which we installed the stair-inspired LED-edged artwork). Workshop/APD's carpet for Warp & Weft meanders down the hall, and James Welling's *Torso 3-6* hangs above the primary bedroom's Ortiz bench.

The primary suite's expansive, enveloping Workshop/APD-designed headboard, neutral palette, and "abstract forest" carpet encourage an atmosphere of quiet, calm, and repose (in keeping with the presence, just outside the windows, of Central Park). The pendant lights and armchair are from Future Perfect. The bath's mirror reflects artist Vik Muniz's take on Richard Avedon's iconic photograph of Marilyn Monroe.

Aware that many of the shots aimed at the basketball hoop would likely miss their mark, we covered the walls and ceiling of the children's playroom in sturdy Astroturf. The overlapping Dune sofas invite comfortable crashing, as do the Afra and Tobia Scarpa–influenced lounge chairs. *You Are Here* is by Saul Sanchez.

THE JOY OF LETTING GO

As noted, we were glad, and most grateful, to have work. But it's no less the case that, in the beginning, there was a space between that which we fantasized about and what actually came over the transom.

Our office was in Manhattan, but if you analyzed our dreams, you'd have told us to pack up and move to LA. We were—are—modernists, who wanted to design and build ground-up residences on decent-sized properties for keenly appreciative clients—houses that, if we'd ever actually gotten to do them, would have been the grandchildren of the Case Study projects produced by Saarinen, Eames, Koenig, Soriano, and others during Southern California's postwar Golden Age. What our firm actually got offered, however, was very different: jobs remodeling historic Nantucket beach houses, and classic prewar apartments on New York's Upper East and West Sides.

This was…perplexing. Apart from the fact that neither of us were practitioners in the classical tradition, both the Nantucket and New York typologies were possessed of very strong, recognizable design languages that—if not exactly inflexible—did not invite deviation. Indeed, as regards Nantucket, local regulations dictated what one could or could not build.

We won't say that we weren't a bit disappointed. But if our opportunities didn't align with our passions, we were nonetheless keen to inject our passions into our opportunities. As architectural designers enamored of clean, edited spaces, we questioned how we might introduce a more modern agenda into projects that weren't obviously suited to one. Partly there was a measure of arrogance involved, as we were young and had no wish to be deprived of our "voice." Even so, it remained a design problem rooted in an entirely practical consideration: How does one exist in a historical context in a way that comfortably reflects the realities of contemporary life? And so we set about crafting designs that reflected our personalities and predilections, in circumstances that were their opposite in style and spirit. After all, we reassured ourselves, if that wasn't what our clients really wanted, they wouldn't have come to us, right?

Fortunately—and this proved decisive—we had developed a way of thinking about architecture that had less to do with the specifics of style, typology, and even structure, and was more engaged with the question of how people used, and navigated, space. Thus the actual aesthetic language remained less important than the relationships between pieces, and whether or not they were organic and, in the end, holistic. Style, to our way of thinking, was the clothing; the plan was the individual, and if we created a well-balanced and proportioned body, it could conceivably be dressed in anything.

We had also put a great deal of thought into constructing a rigorous yet pliable process that let us approach any manner of design challenge in a consistent, organized fashion: one that interleaved the micro and macro, and drilled down from broad strokes to fine-grained issues of execution and detail. The projects might be diverse. The mode of working remained consistent.

It would be easy, and not entirely inaccurate, to describe the work we did as "traditional without, contemporary within": "old meets new" might be one's at-a-glance characterization. But that would shortchange the discernment and, indeed, respect with which we addressed the preexisting architecture. Considering the homes in which we were asked to work, our approach was instead to enhance—to ask: How can we preserve or amplify the essential character of what exists, while also bringing forward its latent potential?

One of our very first New York projects was set in an expressionistic building on that cosmopolitan rampart known as Central Park West, in an apartment with details that were the acme of prewar elegance *(p. 298)*. Our clients had specified a very contemporary, flexible program at odds with their home's history. So we chose to treat the apartment's perimeter as a kind of classical wrapper, into which we inserted a capacious piece of contemporary "furniture": a pristine box, enclosing all of the public and private living spaces. By treating the home as a modern gift set in a historic package, we were able to bridge the space between two epochs (and their different sensibilities) by ringing a change on the concept of a "jewel box residence" to represent both its old and new iterations.

Some people begin their professional lives doing precisely what they dreamed of doing and continue on that path to the very end. More often, however, one starts out with a specific vision, crashes into a very different reality, and then is faced with reconciling the two. That's what happened to us, and though it wasn't what we wanted, it proved to be an extraordinary bit of good fortune. Had our first gig been a neo–Case Study house in the Hollywood Hills, we might never have found the wherewithal to be imaginative and adaptable. We might never have learned, in a deep way, about architectural history: the austere beauty of its rigors, the elegance of its languages, and how both could be applied to a wide range of new work. We might never have been challenged to move beyond the safe, the expected—everything that came off the drafting table might look pretty much the same. And as that last consideration suggests, we might never have developed the reputation for formal diversity that has led so many clients to trust us with so many different kinds of work. Getting handed what we didn't want has enabled the firm to do so much more than we ever imagined possible. Not having it our way might well be the best thing that ever befell us, as designers and, perhaps, as individuals. As our grandparents might have put it: Who knew?

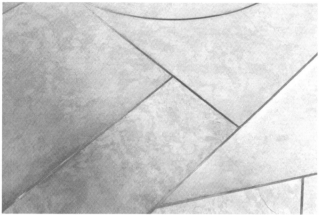

This full-floor apartment, in a new building on Manhattan's Upper East Side, began life as a four-bedroom residence—gutted at our clients' request, recast as a two-bedroom, and divided into discrete public and private zones, both accessed from a new foyer entered directly from the elevator **(ABOVE)**. Visitors are greeted by an Hubert Le Gall mirror and a wall console from Fernando Mastrangelo. For the entry to the public side **(OPPOSITE)** we designed a Deco-style decorative pattern, rendered in brass-inlaid polished concrete, then carried it upward to craft a glass-and-brass screen that frames a view of the living room. A highly polished black-mirrored ceiling completes the experience with theatrical glamour. The artwork, by David Salle, is opposite the portal to the dining/kitchen area.

The dining table—just one of the residence's many singular pieces—was created by the Warsaw-born, UK-based multidisciplinary designer Marcin Rusak by preserving a cornucopia of florals in a jet-black pool of resin. It is paired with Lazzarini Pickering chairs upholstered in Nella Vetrina suede, providing a bold pop of color in an otherwise monochromatic kitchen.

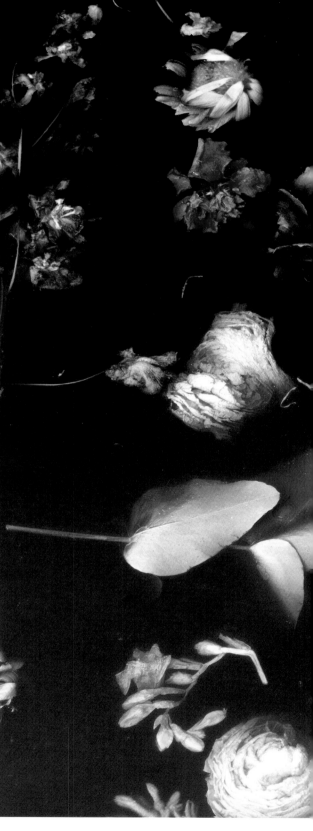

The effect is similar to that of a Dutch still life, and extends the motif—established in the entry—of aesthetic history reimagined for the twenty-first century. Each carefully curated piece embodies the client's passion for artistry and craftsmanship.

Formerly a bedroom, the kitchen/dining room remains as elegantly pristine as a Madison Avenue *joaillier's* establishment and expresses our desire to introduce a curvilinear language into the sharp-angled geometries of the architecture (exemplified by the custom Niamh Barry chandelier). The living and dining areas are delineated by a portal comprised of a pair of custom-designed vitrines, the glass softly frosted by embedded mesh screens. The museum-quality objects and furnishings include a coffee table by Erwan Boulloud, which captures in brass and onyx the effects of raindrops striking a pond's surface, William Georgis's Whalebone sofa, and a pair of Embrace chairs by Michael Berman.

Turn your back to the dining table, and this is what you see: an expansive living room, constructed from the original dining and living spaces, zoned for relaxing and entertaining (at right), television watching (on the left), and working (at the Workshop/APD-designed desk by the rear wall). The swooping, wavelike ceiling—again, a contemporary take on the rosettes, beams, and mouldings of yesteryear—helps to articulate the two sitting areas and, in sympathy with the organic furnishings, softens and sensualizes the box. Hervé Van der Straeten designed the pendant above the circular occasional table by the window; the sculptural lamp is by Pia-Maria Raeder.

The expansive primary suite, crafted from two preexisting bedrooms, is cozy, comfortable, and luxurious with walls upholstered in soft, sound-dampening fabrics. The night tables, dresser, and a desk were designed by our office and capture the project's subtle sense of rich materiality. The sofa, by Patrick Naggar for Pucci, is paired with Lindsey Adelman wall sconces, and a round Miya Ando artwork hangs above the bed.

This residence sits atop a multiacre site in Westchester County, at an elevation high enough to afford views of the Manhattan skyline, some 35 miles to the south. It represents an aspect of our firm's aesthetic characterized as Progressive Vernacular, which is, simply put, a contemporary interpretation of tradition. Here the style is reflected in the combination of vernacular elements—a cross gable and standing-seam roof, shiplap siding, stone quarried on site—with large expanses of glass and compositions reflective of modern modes of living (notably an entry "gasket" that affords views directly through the house).

LEFT: The perfectly symmetrical entry zone features an inviting tableau comprised of multicolored pendant lamps above a shapely console table. **OPPOSITE and ABOVE:** Beneath a gabled ceiling finished in white oak, the great room—incorporating kitchen, dining, and living areas—faces due west, flooding the volumetric space with a warm glow in all seasons. The Tod Von Mertens wood dining table is paired with Ochre chandeliers.

OPPOSITE: The great room's living area reflects our clients' desire for a home with a strong connection to the natural world. **ABOVE:** The house remains open, not only to the landscape but to its various components, reflected here in the view from the living area, across an exterior zone, to a three-season sitting room. **RIGHT:** The fireplace's chamfer detail repeats in many of the house's decorative design components, producing a unity of vision that individualizes the residence's architecture.

The main stair and a vestibule with coat closets and a powder room introduce the warmth of the near-ubiquitous white oak that wraps and enfolds the house's various spaces. We describe this as the "quilting" of materials, which enables us to wring imaginative configurations from a simple, limited palette. **FOLLOWING PAGES:** Rather than treating the three-season room as an appendage, we incorporated it into the mass of the house, thereby dematerializing the distinction between the landscape and the architecture.

Only the thinnest of transparent membranes marks the interior/ exterior boundary in the primary bedroom and bath. Beyond the glazing, the landscaping falls away into what seems like unexpurgated nature but is in fact the product of months of excavation and sitework.

The game room (and its well-curated bar) are on the residence's lower level and open onto the pool deck (seen at left on page 84). The polished concrete floor is the structure's one departure from white oak, a concession to wet feet. The pool table was created with Blatt Billiards, with a custom finish and felt to complement the décor.

The fully glazed gable form below marks the rear elevation of the residence's great room. The staircase leading down to the pool, at left, begins at the space between the great room and the three-season sitting room. Sculpting these areas for outdoor activity, and integrating them naturally into the residential experience, proved perhaps the greatest design challenge, and the one that delivered the greatest joy.

FOLLOWING PAGES: This view reveals the primary suite, extending out horizontally from the back of the house, followed by its semi-public zone, and, beyond it, the long volume enclosing the great room—all of it nestled naturally and inevitably into the landscape.

This duplex apartment, on Manhattan's Fifth Avenue, sits north of the Metropolitan Museum of Art in a building of singular eccentricity. Its most distinctive feature is the dynamic, swirling stair we created to unite the two floors. Architecture tends to be planar, and stairs offer a cinematic opportunity to transform space, to change one's perspective and, indeed, orientation. This one, a ribbon of self-supporting bent steel finished in wood and plaster and set against a muscular wall of rough-cut travertine, terminates with uncommon grace—the splayed ends, sensual and welcoming, invite one to enter and ascend.

Opposite the stair, the bar forms an inviting portal to
the main living area. For the installation behind the
sink, we commissioned Ethereal Atelier, artisans who
embed branches in rippling sheets of liquid bronze,
creating an elegant, appropriate complement to both
the lightly figured marble and the presence, beyond the
panoramic floor-to-ceiling windows, of Central Park.

RIGHT: Past the double-height space defined by the stair and bar, we see the living room, the first of the three distinct zones that comprise the apartment's great room. **ABOVE:** The diminutive yet highly functional and densely programmed office nook continues the pale, organic material palette characteristic of the residence's grander spaces.

TOP: The dining area is sited between the living and family "rooms" in the loftlike open-plan space; we crafted a mid-century-modern-style ceiling detail above the table and chairs to strengthen the sense of differentiation. **ABOVE and LEFT:** The kitchen adjoins the family area and incorporates the same highly reflective Venetian plaster finish on the ceiling, which captures light and makes all of the spaces feel taller.

OPPOSITE and ABOVE: While the lower floor incorporates two baths, three children's rooms, and a playroom, the upstairs is entirely the province of the primary suite. The bedroom, which overlooks the park, is separated from the stair landing by a wall of glass, which allows light to enter the apartment's recesses by day and can be curtained off, for privacy, at night.

RIGHT: Directly opposite the top of the stair, across the landing from the bedroom, lies the primary bath and dressing room, a capacious stone-and-wood-clad chamber with abundant closet and vanity space.

HAND

In a 1948 speech to the House of Commons, Winston Churchill slightly revised George Santayana's famous observation, saying that "those who fail to learn from history are condemned to repeat it." As we discovered working on our New York and Nantucket projects, this maxim remains especially applicable to making architecture, though not absolutely in the ways that one might imagine. Had we attempted to work in historic styles without first making a deep dive into their origins, we'd have simply parroted their surfaces. But precisely because we *did* learn from the historical precedents we investigated, those early projects reinterpreted the ideas and intentions of their predecessors in ways that suited the present-day predilections of our clients. The key lay in making personal connections with those earlier styles, and we found different ways of doing so—most effectively via the idea of *hand*.

"Hand" is, admittedly, one of those words architects like to toss around, not always with care. But it has meaning, and it matters. It refers, of course, to craft, the use of hand-making and natural materials to invest an interior or structure with character and soul. But there is also what might be described as a "hand of the mind and spirit": architecture and design that is so intently considered in so many ways—concept, narrative, imagination, influence—that it delivers an intimate, thoroughgoing satisfaction that is the equivalent of the pleasures offered by hand-making. As we moved on from Shingle Style cottages and Deco aeries, what we learned came with us. And we frequently found ourselves bridging the space between history and modernity—and in projects very different in character—with both the actual and spiritual manifestations of hand.

Perhaps the earliest instance of this was a stairway we created for a loft residence in New York's Tribeca district *(p. 298)*. At a glance it is aggressively modern, a sleek ribbon of perforated steel. It's also what might be described as the seminal Workshop/APD effort. Yet the object was inspired by the most unlikely of sources, one we discovered at the Metropolitan Museum of Art: the staircase from Cassiobury Park, Herfordshire, an elaborately carved affair featuring multiple natural elements rendered in oak, elm, and pine, attributed to Edward Pearce, and completed around 1680. Even if it's not your thing, it's an absolutely stunning piece of work, as bravura an example of hand as you're ever likely to encounter.

We don't build that way today. But seeing the stair as we conceptualized the loft, it ignited a line of speculation: could we work with a single, unmistakably modern material and transform it, via an organic language, into something with the same richness of character that Pearce achieved in the seventeenth century? From this sprang the abstract vegetal patterns laser-cut into the steel, the gracefully turned "newel post" that encircled the column at the stair's lower terminus. Twenty-first-century Manhattan loft living is a modern trope; with the stair, we found a way to introduce historical precedent, and the timeless consolations of hand, in a modern way. That resonance, we suspect, is what has attracted so many people to this design moment—and led us to wonder as well how it might be amplified to the scale of a project.

Perhaps we were more open to it, but inspiration seemed to arrive from multiple corners. Engaged to design a lake house in rural New York *(p. 118)*—our first, and a different breed of cat, to be sure, from a New England beach house—we studied the buildings at the Stone Barn Center in nearby Pocantico Hills.

The Rockefellers, who'd owned the land, imported some of the agrarian structures from France; they were simple volumes, with hand-crafted details on the roofs and dormers, but in the rural context their simplicity and honesty, the evident care and conviction with which they'd been executed, impressed and moved us. From this example, the contemporized design of our lake house flowed naturally and organically.

Back in Manhattan, in a spacious but somewhat featureless Upper East Side apartment, we completely gutted the interior and replaced it with two precedents, in a kind of capsule history of twentieth-century New York design: the public rooms drew inspiration from the Deco glamour of Donald Deskey's Radio City Music Hall interiors; the private areas we invested with the austere mid-century elegance of Mies van der Rohe's Seagram building *(p. 61)*. By applying "hand of the mind and spirit," we were able to see the relationship between the two periods, and marry them effectively and with a sense of fun.

There are times when one transgresses against one's self-image, understanding that something transformative awaits on transgression's far shore. Maybe we weren't entirely conscious of it as it happened. But our pursuit of a personal, twenty-first-century interpretation of hand, of a modern design idiom that uncurls, like a serpent from a charmer's basket, out of the past, helped to liberate us from our assumptions regarding what we *should* be doing, and gave us permission to embrace our architectural heart's desire. And you know what? It was fine to fall from our first idea of grace. Sometimes the better part of wisdom—and good design—is letting things be what they are.

For this exceptionally grand beach house in the Bahamas, the brief was simple—and double-edged: the owners requested a destination that could host the most formal events, yet also be comfortable enough for flip-flops in every room. In the arrival courtyard, broad stone pavers cross a reflecting pool to arrive at an eleven-foot-tall front door. The blue-green slate slabs on the reflecting pool's floor form a rectilinear patchwork that contrasts with the organic character of the lushly planted beds and abstract sculptural element, *Veiled in a Dream*, by Wendell Castle.

Upon entering, one looks directly across the indoor/outdoor living room, with its custom twenty-foot-long facing sofas, to the deck and, beyond it, the sea (as seen on pages 104–5). The sculpture at the window is by Nick van Woert, and a work by Jan Albers hangs above the bar.

On one side of the living room, a bar is flanked by pocket doors that connect to the house's subordinate spaces. The enameled, multicolor lava stone coffee table by Emmanuel Babled encapsulates the spirit of the project: an intersection of materials and forms.

To create privacy and elevate functionality, the kitchen's primary wall features windows that are narrow and discreetly placed. The twenty-foot-long island accommodates food preparation on one side and seating on the other. As elsewhere in the residence, high ceilings prevail, and a multiglobe Equalizer pendant light from The Future Perfect helps to bring the space down to a more intimate scale.

With pocket doors on three sides, the dining room is effectively an outdoor experience that can be enclosed when necessary. The exterior connection is strengthened by the floor's unfilled travertine pavers, which also appear on the villa's outside walls. Workshop/APD's massive Schism dining table is broken into two slabs, so that smaller groups can dine comfortably on one or another side of the divide. The buoy-like Nao Tamura chandelier is an appropriate accompaniment to the oceanfront setting.

LEFT: No, that is not a flat-screen TV in the family room but rather *Spring Plunge*, an Eric Zener photograph printed on silver leaf that casts a glow visible from as far away as the dining table (see page 108). Gregory Siff's *Make Fishes* hangs to the right of the bookshelves. **BELOW:** Custom-painted surfboards serve as artworks in the adjacent media room, which features architectural Vibia ceiling pendant lights.

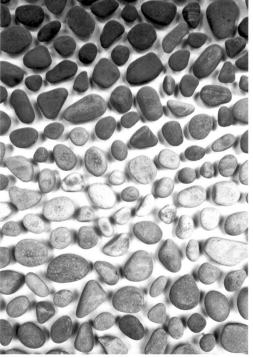

OPPOSITE: Each of the house's two staircases incorporates a curvilinear sand element that showcases a large Boaz Vaadia installation, an effective means of bringing together the natural and human-made landscapes. Custom Lollipop pendants from Lasvit add light, color, casualness, and scale. **ABOVE:** An arresting installation of hand-selected stones by artist Charles Patrick, in the second-floor gallery overlooking the entry court, uses hundreds of individual pieces to render an aerial view of the beachscape on the other side of the house.

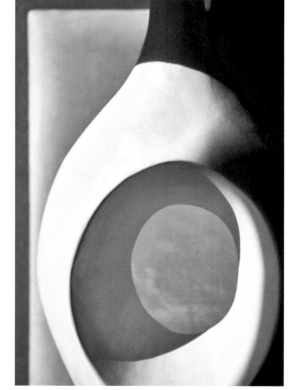

ABOVE: Workshop/APD designed the primary suite's sleeping ensemble; beyond the white oak wall, on which hangs Enrique Santana's *Mediterranean (Triptych)*, the bath is to the right **(OPPOSITE, ABOVE)**, the dressing area is at left. Here, as elsewhere, the unpainted walls are finished in decorative plaster, which bestows an overlay of solidity in the beautiful yet fluid environment. Custom-crafted bedside lamps capture the character of sea life.

The negative-edge pool scales up the design concept begun in the house's forecourt, with varying shades of slate forming a Mondrian-esque rhythm on its floor. The seemingly random configuration of palm trees—which were, in fact, carefully placed—helps to privatize the pool and give scale to the view.

This house, overlooking a lake in a discreet hamlet within the town of Lewisboro, some fifty miles from Manhattan, is the oldest project to be found in these pages. We were engaged to create a "classic" lake house nestled in the woods. Yet while the front, two-story elevation suggests the historic regional barns that served as inspiration, the entry reveals not only a three-story structure but a modern interpretation of a vernacular style.

The living room exposes the house's emphasis on texture and pattern, evident from floor (the checkerboard hide rug) to ceiling (where we flogged the beams with chains until they looked sufficiently weathered). As we wanted the décor to feel diverse and collected rather than of a piece, the interiors came together slowly as our team searched for objects with the appropriate character. The firewood is stacked in diamond-shaped compartments reminiscent of wine storage.

The kitchen's white oak boards and pale marble contrast elegantly with the Noguchi-esque live-edge dining table. To achieve the light and drama of a soaring cathedral ceiling, we cut a space out of the second-floor primary suite, into which we inserted a Jean Royère–inspired chandelier by Designheure.

123

OPPOSITE and LEFT: Believing that a dead zone is the enemy of effective and efficient design, we seek to activate the spaces between rooms with habitable circulation spines (often the coziest "rooms" in a scheme). **ABOVE:** The primary bedroom balances the rustic—notably a soaring mantelpiece built from stone quarried on site—and the refined, evident in the fabrics and furnishings.

What appears upon arrival to be a two-story house adds a lower level in back, on the elevation overlooking the lake. Here we added a mélange of outdoor sitting areas, covered and exposed, and united the two projecting wings with a glass bridge that floats above a reflecting pool.

Though the site and setting exude serenity, this repose was earned with two years of labor involving the removal of large quantities of stone (much of which became a raw material for the house). Rather than more traditional cedar, the exterior is finished in shingles of white oak, which ages erratically and gives the residence a timeworn, old-world character that is reminiscent of the vernacular structures that inspired us.

HISTORY—PAST AND PRESENT

Should you find yourself in London, treat yourself to a visit to the Natural History Museum on Cromwell Road. The original structure, the landmark 1881 Waterhouse Building, exemplifies the agreeable mix of stately reserve and haunted-house menace so typical of institutional Victorian architecture. The story, however, does not end there. Connected to the Waterhouse, via a slender glass gasket, is C. F. Møller Architects' twenty-first-century Darwin Centre; and though it could not be more different in style from its predecessor, the colossal, cocoon-like object, built in part to hold the museum's collection of specimens—seventeen million insects, three million plants—seems entirely "in keeping," as the English say. Its scale perfectly captures the vastness of the enterprise; the design draws on a form from the natural world to project the spirit of protection and transformation.

Early in our career, we had an opportunity to create something similar (on a much more modest scale) when the firm won the commission to design a 25,000-square-foot commercial addition to the nineteenth-century Marine Corps Commandant's Residence at New York's Brooklyn Navy Yard *(p. 298)*. The residence itself struck us as an object nearly radioactive with history—of the mighty waterfront, the city's storied mercantile past, American maritime supremacy, and even Brooklyn's elegant domestic architecture— and we had no wish to make a "Great Statement" at the house's expense. Our proposal stressed reverence, setting the modern building at a remove and partially concealed from the street, and affording the historic original ample breathing room. The connection between the two: a discreet architectural "hyphen."

We'd been concerned that, as institutional-architecture novices, the Navy Yard folks wouldn't trust us with so important an assignment. But we got the job, and discovered something essential: how beneficial it can be to both history *and* modernity if the space between them is bridged with intelligence, imagination, and flair.

It has always been our ambition to apply the multiple lessons of any project to our subsequent work, and what we discovered scaling the steep learning curve of the Brooklyn Navy Yard proved exceptionally useful when we were called upon to preserve, and add to, historic components—a miner's cottage in Aspen *(p. 144)* and a Tudor mansion in Connecticut *(p. 298)*, to name two. In each of these homes, the shades of past and present intermingled, took each other's measure, stepped forward and stood back; in each, "the space between" is filled with the spirit of engagement, an impulse toward mutual exploration—and the desire for an architectural sum greater than its (old or new) parts.

The lessons learned, moreover, are not only applicable to projects in which "the preexisting" and "the newly added" play distinct and clearly separate roles. If this particular state of affairs presents itself with relative infrequency, it is also the case that a majority of the projects our office undertakes involve some sort of engagement with the bygone. A prime example: In virtually any apartment renovation, for better or worse, a surprise awaits; you can open up a wall and find a structural impediment that completely neutralizes your intentions, or discover a historic relic so remarkable and unexpected that it inspires you to go in an entirely different creative direction (a circumstance both tantalizing and terrifying).

What's more, the interweaving of old and new need not only involve the tangible. The Navy Yard project, as noted, was influenced as much by the romance of Brooklyn's mythos and history (and our complicated responses to it) as the Marine Corps Commandant's Residence itself or our client's program. As is evident in so many projects in these pages, the space between what exists in the real world—the quotidian facts at hand—and the shifting, textured cloud of old legend that surrounds it can represent the most fertile creative terrain. Architecture is an expensive proposition, and we take pains at all times to contend with what is in front of us. But neither do we forget those most famous of lines, from William Faulkner's *Requiem for a Nun*: "The past is never dead. It's not even past."

An addendum: Even in the most carefully considered project, it remains essential not to cross the line into overdetermination—to create architecture that presents an experience that's seductive and pleasing, but doesn't micromanage that experience to the extent that the end-user has nothing to contribute, that robs one of the opportunity to participate. We strive and strive to build narratives into homes that the residents can complete with inhabitation. If a homeowner can "finish" what we've done with his or her presence, that is the best kind of success.

This duplex constitutes a project within a project: it is an apartment we created in a former industrial building, one that our firm was engaged to reimagine as a residential complex. Originally three small studios with sleeping lofts, we combined the spaces and gave the entirety distinction with a singular element: an organic translucent mezzanine, set against a walnut library wall that serves as a showcase for the family's history. The object in the living room is a decommissioned missile.

We created a mezzanine that is thin, light, and immaterial enough to be at once Calder-esque in character yet unobtrusive, with vertical rib elements that not only create divisions within the display wall to showcase the clients' books and objects, but also support the mezzanine floor, stair, and glass panels. From a compressed height of roughly seven feet, the space explodes upward to roughly twice that upon entry into the residence's public zones.

The living and kitchen areas enjoy a full ceiling height of about fourteen feet and, in contrast with the mezzanine and display wall, remain simple in conception and execution. The kitchen can be fully enclosed by sliding panels, if so desired; Counter-Evolution stools contribute pops of bright yellow. Our concerns regarding the low-slung areas were allayed upon discovering that the compression worked as long as it remained largely confined to circulation and/or private (as opposed to social) areas.

The residence's domestic spaces lie beyond the display wall, which separates the public and private zones. Hudson Furniture crafted the live-edge headboard in the primary bedroom, an organic complement to the highly distinctive Taylor Llorente armchair. The ladder leads up to a writing nook, set in the space above the primary bath/dressing room. **FOLLOWING PAGES:** The mezzanine and library wall add visual, experiential, and spatial complexity to what began as a trio of narrow cookie-cutter studios.

ASPEN SKI RETREAT

ABOVE: Incredibly enough, Harold Ross, the legendary founding editor of *The New Yorker* magazine, was born in this miner's cabin—its traditional exterior contravened by our interior renovation **(LEFT)**—in Aspen, Colorado's historic west end, in 1892. **OPPOSITE:** A modern two-story component, its eccentric window framing a view of Shadow Mountain, sits behind the historic home (concealed from the street by trees). We restored the landmarked original and clad the new addition in slats of ipe wood, which has weathered to a discreet dove gray.

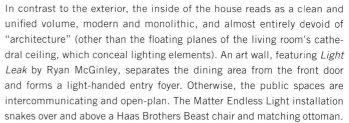

In contrast to the exterior, the inside of the house reads as a clean and unified volume, modern and monolithic, and almost entirely devoid of "architecture" (other than the floating planes of the living room's cathedral ceiling, which conceal lighting elements). An art wall, featuring *Light Leak* by Ryan McGinley, separates the dining area from the front door and forms a light-handed entry foyer. Otherwise, the public spaces are intercommunicating and open-plan. The Matter Endless Light installation snakes over and above a Haas Brothers Beast chair and matching ottoman.

The gray stone island, which separates the kitchen from the dining area, features a movable component set on casters, which can be pulled out to serve as a spot for enjoying casual meals, then pushed back in to form a solid volume for family dining, formal serving, and entertaining.

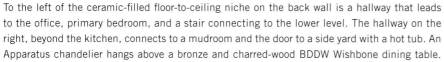

To the left of the ceramic-filled floor-to-ceiling niche on the back wall is a hallway that leads to the office, primary bedroom, and a stair connecting to the lower level. The hallway on the right, beyond the kitchen, connects to a mudroom and the door to a side yard with a hot tub. An Apparatus chandelier hangs above a bronze and charred-wood BDDW Wishbone dining table.

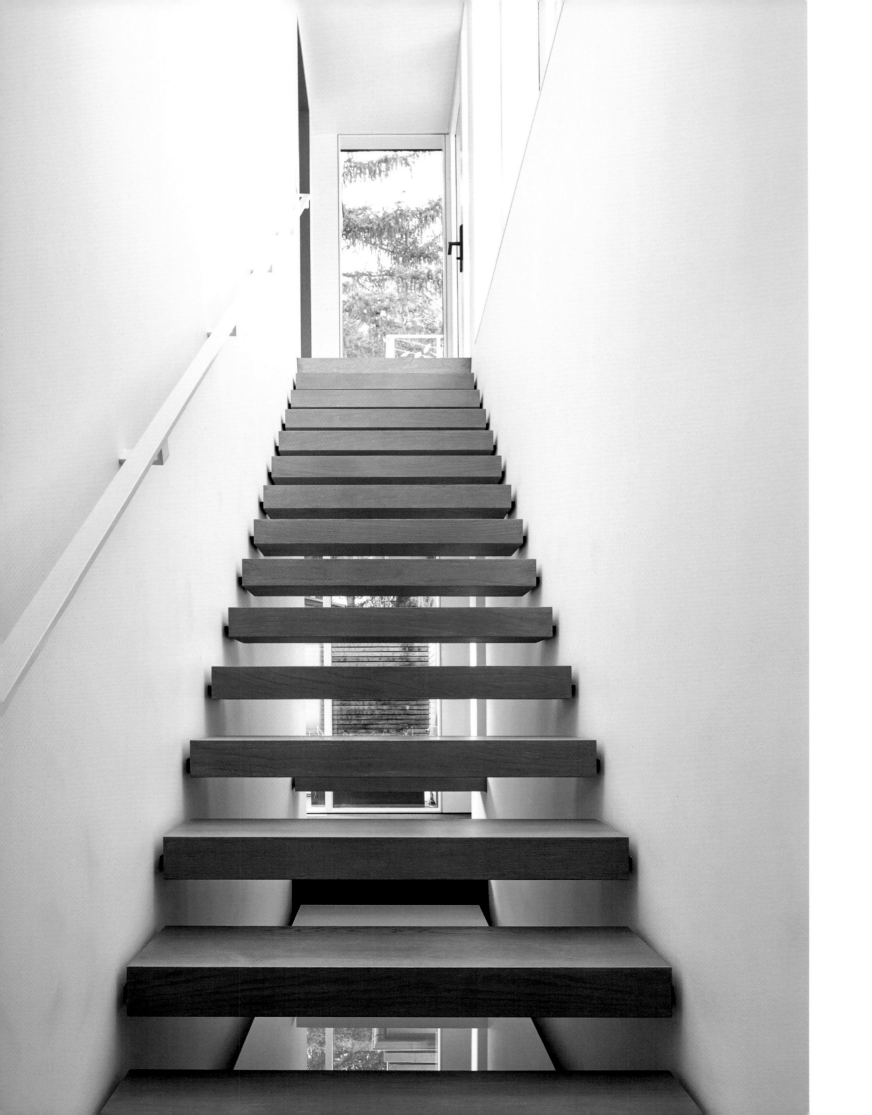

A stair **(OPPOSITE)** both solid and ephemeral leads up to the second-floor primary suite **(THIS PAGE)**. The walls and ceiling are finished in a concrete plaster, the mottled, light-absorbing effect of which complements the warmth of the white oak floor. The Workshop/APD-designed live-edge bench, a collaboration with Uhuru, is paired with a dangling Niamh Barry light sculpture.

LEFT: A cozy space beside the stair does double duty as an office and music room. **OPPOSITE:** The thoughtfully conceived mudroom features individual lockers for equipment storage and an exceptionally sturdy bench for removing ski boots. We chose a natural material palette that subtly recalls the experience of the rustic west while remaining light, crisp, and distinctly modern.

153

To add needed square footage without exceeding the limits imposed by the local building code, we excavated a capacious basement space that incorporates a media room, sauna and bath, and three bedrooms, one with custom-designed and crafted bunk beds. The relaxed yet chic décor, and window wells that draw down natural light, mitigate the semi-subterranean condition.

NATURAL COMPANIONS

There's an old saying: Cats and dogs are natural enemies. The same might be said of architects and interior designers. This wariness is evident in the way that each typically handles the other's discipline.

Yet cats and dogs can be great companions, their typically contrasting personalities complementing each other in ways that, more often than not, bind them tightly together—and, of course, so it can be with architects and interior designers. Our architects can design a house, let's say, that expresses a lucid, compelling vision from the big picture to the smallest details—but a skilled designer might have a better handle on how that house's occupants might actually like to inhabit it. Thus a close collaboration, from commencement to completion, produces an outcome that expresses an unforced consistency of conception tectonically *and* decoratively, with each discipline supporting and encouraging the other.

We were trained as architects, and that's how we began our professional lives. But as we devoted ever more time to thinking about and working with interiors, the firm ended up with an aesthetic version of mission creep, and ventured into the space between architecture and decoration. As another old saying goes, the lessons you learn are the ones you never forget—i.e., we made a lot of mistakes. But the lessons have proven concrete, and durable. Among them: Don't overdo the architecture to such a degree that there's no room for decoration. Preserve the architectural intent while infusing it with livability. Not least: Keep in mind that interior design is, not infrequently, architecture at a different scale.

The last point reflects a significant historical continuum: many great architects also designed decorative objects and furniture—surely Le Corbusier is better known for his globally ubiquitous LC2 sofas and chairs than for Villa Savoye—and many great decorators, notably in France in the interwar years, crafted comprehensive interiors with multifunctional elements that amounted to buildings in miniature. What we have discovered is that the scaling up or down of decorative elements can be actual, as when a custom furniture piece replicates the forms and details of its surroundings, or thematic, taking the overarching *idea* of the grand scheme and playing it out in decorative motifs that capture its spirit. The thought, invariably, isn't to draw a line—to say, "Here's where architecture ends and decoration begins"—but rather to blur the distinction: whether something happens at the scale of a room, a chair, or a hand, unity (even the unity of contrast) remains essential.

Another, most interesting discovery, one that increased our respect for the interior design profession: while it can be relatively painless to create architecture, as the craft seems a bit like voodoo to the uninitiated, the instant you switch to picking a dining chair,

the easiest client might become the most difficult—because *now* you're dealing with something that person understands, touches, and has experienced. You would be amazed by the number of clients who happily acquiesced to the most audacious architectural schemes, then lapsed into an advanced case of analysis paralysis when faced with a choice of chandeliers. The finesse required to lead people, not only to a decorative decision but to the *right* decision, is something the best designers possess in abundance, and many architects—so used to having their way—cannot manage.

Accordingly, Workshop/APD's interior design directors attend early client meetings on every new commission, an aspect of our process that ensures that all departments move forward simultaneously and transparently. More critically, having a better understanding of the fundamental differences between the disciplines, we no longer try to compel the firm's interior designers to think and act like architects. The particular linear process that we pursue doesn't work for designers, who develop and refine their ideas and motifs in a more intuitive, inspiration-driven manner, one which involves much back and forth with their clients.

To tell one on ourselves: It took perhaps half a decade to give up on trying to make the designers do it our way. But once we did, our projects became more balanced, more cohesive, and—to use a most un-architectural word—prettier.

Despite the historic local penchant for Spanish and Italianate tradition, the vein of white-on-white mid-century modern architecture in fact runs deep in Palm Beach, where this house was designed by a disciple of Richard Meier. But if the style itself remains enduringly popular, the ways in which people choose to "live modern" fluctuate with the times. We were enlisted to reprogram and redecorate this residence, which was modern without, traditional within. We began in the entry, by installing new lighting and crafting a furniture tableau that establishes the decorative tone.

As the owners had three rooms they seldom used, we worked to maximize the house's function-ality while maintaining an elevated but inviting, casual-swank spirit—a gambit evident in the enormous living room, which we scaled by crafting multiple overlapping conversation zones.

The room features furniture pieces from Holly Hunt, Christian Liaigre, and Minotti, among others. Our office designed the free-form marble cocktail tables, and the entirety sits atop a Perennials gray Tibetan Knot Landscape rug and beneath John Procario's Freeform Series Light Sculpture II.

OPPOSITE: Perle Fine painted the living room's large and colorful canvas. THIS PAGE: The dining and family rooms traded functions, which made the transition from cocktails in the living room to a sit-down dinner more natural and free-flowing. The chandelier above the dining table is by David Weeks Studio, and a Ross Bleckner painting hangs above the Mobili Cantù cupboard.

THIS PAGE, OPPOSITE, and FOLLOWING PAGES: The principal architectural intervention was made in the kitchen, where a huge, battleship-size island was exchanged for three faceted quartzite volumes, for cooking, serving, and storage. The floor-to-ceiling pivoting glass panes enable different degrees of communication between the spaces.

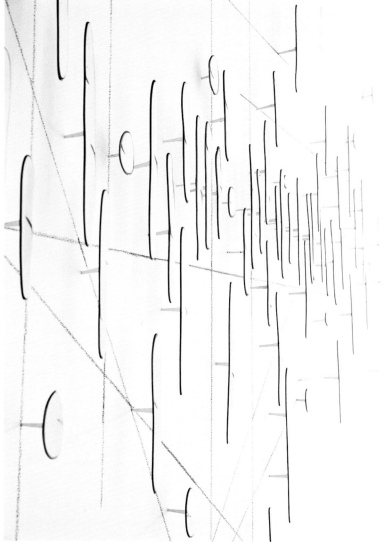

OPPOSITE: The artwork above the primary bedroom dresser is in fact a framed Hermès scarf—one of our client's favorite objects. **RIGHT:** An installation of porcelain pieces on pins, arranged in situ and connected via hand-drawn lines by the artist.

This very handsome Spanish Colonial courtyard house, with its inviting view of Pebble Beach, was designed in 1925 by the noted Pasadena architect Reginald Davis Johnson. The residence was restored some years before we were engaged to work on it, and our brief largely involved interior decoration. While our scheme acknowledged the house's aesthetic origins, particularly as regards the neutral-in-to-brown color palette, we moved the décor subtly forward in time by introducing vintage mid-century modern pieces as well as contemporary objects.

The austere elegance of the dining room arose from the slate floor, at once rustic and refined. Both the pendants and the table beneath them (paired with Olofsson dining chairs) are from Holly Hunt. The free-form slate slabs also facilitate a natural aesthetic connection to the adjoining exterior court.

Though our firm was principally tasked with designing the interiors, we undertook architectural interventions in the baths, mudroom, and kitchen, separated from the dining room by wood-frame divided-light doors. Dark and neutral toned woods, and lightly figured stone, simply deployed in a minimal rectilinear scheme, meshed naturally with the residence's foundational style.

The library's split-faced stacked stone walls, muscular timbered ceiling, and slate floor give the room an appealing, rough-hewn character. We leaned into this—with a custom travertine cocktail table—and softened it, with upholstered furnishings and a plush rug. Though the black-and-white photograph above the sofa features Big Sur, the view from behind the desk faces the scenic seventeen-mile drive stretching from Monterey to Carmel, a slice of paradise first developed in 1892.

As interesting as the architectural precedents are the regional decorative influences, which led us to feature overscaled, faintly primitive, and/or naturalistic pieces. These include the Wyllis nightstands in the primary bedroom, designed by Arthur de Mattos Casas, and featuring wood frames incorporating drawers and doors of unfilled travertine. These remarkable design objects perfectly encapsulate the spirit of the project, which combines natural elements, often roughly finished, with the utmost refinement and elegance. The complementary Tiberius lamps are from Danny Kaplan Studio.

HOW CLOSE IS FAR ENOUGH?

One of Workshop/APD's more intriguing projects involved an ultra-modern loft space, in an iconic building designed by a world-famous architect, with 270-degree views up and down the Hudson River *(p. 200)*. These stunning vistas were the glass-box apartment's main attraction—*and* its great challenge, one that afflicts many similar urban aeries: while you're looking out, others look in. In this instance, though the principal panoramic exposure faced westward across the waterway, the windows to the north and south were mere yards from the neighbors, creating a veritable voyeur's paradise. The question presented itself: How to resolve the space between another's eyes and one's own?

Our first gambit was counterintuitive: competing (in a small way) with the view. There is the received notion that, if you purchase a property for what's out the window, you need to lean into it. But as any fish can tell you, a few colored rocks and strands of seaweed won't change the essential character of a fishbowl: The sculptural television we set directly in front of the west-facing window gave the living room a sense of self-containment while subtracting nothing from the big picture. On the south side, where we located the primary suite, a light layer of Corian shelves—set against the glass, adorned sparingly with eye-catching objects—created privacy without the need for curtains or shades and, by restating the grid pattern of the building across the street, enabled us to take ownership of the world beyond the windows, to make it part of the residential experience. Most significantly, we pulled most of the program away from the glazed perimeter and toward the center, shaping a volume within the volume from which we carved rooms—kitchen, baths, bedrooms—as though taking bites from an apple. The outcome holds privacy and exposure in exquisite balance: preserving the command, the urban majesty, of the views, and ensuring the inward-looking intimacy of an inviolate personal domain.

We've been fortunate in that quite a few of the residences the firm has been asked to design are "view projects." And from the first, we have proceeded from the proposition that, ultimately, in any hand-to-hand competition with the natural (or, for that matter, the picturesquely human-made) world, the architect is bound to lose. But once you've accepted that—once you've stopped thinking of it as a competition—a world of possibility opens up. Whether one chooses to frame the dynamic as concealment versus exposure, looking out versus looking in, or simply as a matter of context, the imaginative interleaving of a work of architecture and its larger circumstances becomes richer, more textured, and more complete.

This formulation extends, moreover, to residences that, for whatever reason, turn their back on their external surroundings—in which the solution derives from interior views. Whenever possible, we try to integrate an original installation of one or another sort into our projects, usually an art piece or architectural moment that animates a particular part of the home and reflects the larger design intention. Typically these installations are small in scale; but when a project is a world unto itself, it can become its heart and soul. In a home we created out of four narrow, nondescript apartments in Manhattan's West Village, the "installation" mushroomed into a fourteen-foot-high, glass-and-steel curvilinear loft overlooking the main living area, a construction that's anchored in the building's structural members yet seems to float as weightlessly as an outsize Calder mobile (p. 134). The loft is multifunctional, to be sure. But as a stage from which to survey the action, and a stand-alone object that evokes surprise and delight, the loft encourages an experiential interplay that fuels the

apartment's independent spirit. You might not want to look out the windows—but with so much going on inside, you don't have to.

Experimenting with interior views taught us a great deal about the manipulation of space—how layering, forced perspective, compression and release, and other such gambits can introduce a quiet but unmistakable sense of drama into even the simplest of homes. Consider, if you will, the ceiling. Many of our clients (especially those in mid-century modern apartments) respond to our interest in dropping their ceilings with shock, horror, and despair. *Maximize the ceiling height!* It's like a battle cry. But as we know from Frank Lloyd Wright, who made something of a specialty of compressed entryways that explode upward into soaring spaces, manipulating the plane above our heads can generate wonder—and it works just as dependably in a 500-square-foot studio as it does in the Guggenheim Museum.

Over the years, we've received what might be described as an experiential education regarding where to draw the line: between too narrow and too wide, too close and too far and, not least, too concealed and too exposed. Much of what we learned arose from trial and error: finding ourselves satisfied with the spatial metrics we'd calculated on the drawing board, only to discover that we'd misjudged distances or proportions when we saw them in three dimensions. Fortuitously, what began as calculation evolved, over time, into intuition, the ability to nimbly sense where lies the sweet spot between two contrasting conditions. In art as in life, we are all drawn to confidence (as opposed to arrogance) and leery of irresolution (not to be confused with deliberation), and the realm of architecture is no exception. If a space feels unresolved, its occupants will never be at home in it. So we're grateful that experience, that great teacher, has given us the confidence to know—intuitively but accurately—where the line gets drawn.

Working in buildings designed by iconic architects—such as this one, on Manhattan's far west side, by Jean Nouvel, famed for its prismatic, jewel-like curtain wall—requires the proverbial delicate balance. On the one hand, you want to answer the needs of your client, in this instance a Midwest-based couple interested in a design that showcases their extensive (and exceptional) art collection. On the other, you want to enhance the architecture rather than compete with or detract from it. Here, it appears that we did almost nothing—and worked very hard at it indeed.

Our gut renovation of this penthouse enabled us to withdraw, to the greatest possible degree, from the windows, then carefully reconsider the plan and the requisite architectural insertions. To craft aesthetic continuity, we brought the geometries developed by Nouvel in his curtain wall into the millwork behind the dining table, and the mirrored range hood in the kitchen captures them as well. The appropriately named Cumulus chandeliers are by Ted Abramczyk.

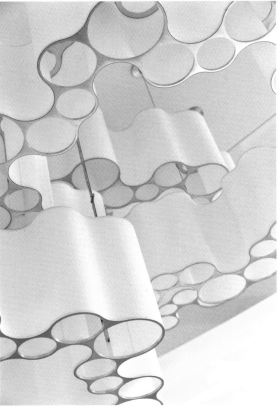

The beauty of Nouvel's design lies in its division of what would typically be an un-obstructed, undifferentiated view into a series of "paintings" of differing sizes and emphases—an ideal condition for our art-loving clients and the gallery-like interiors.

We worked with the owners to place those artworks that would not be susceptible to the sun's depredations in provocative relationships to the view, as with the Kara Walker head at left and Anthony Caro's neo-Giacometti, gazing out the window, at right.

LEFT: A new grand stair, just past the front door, ascends to an expansive roof deck. Given the monumental scale of the spaces, the stunning light, and the sweeping panoramas, luminous white—rendered in lacquer, stone, and paint—was not just appropriate but inevitable. **RIGHT:** A minimalist glass counter, paired with Xert bar chairs, facilitates casual dining with no diminishment of transparency.

RIGHT: In the primary bedroom, Serge Mouille's iconic five-arm Spider lamp, and the base of the Lane H63 console table from Minotti, provide jolts of black. Our office designed the window seat, and if there are more places to perch here than in the typical bedroom, well, there's a reason. *Nude with Lemons*, by Jonathan Gardner, adorns the wall. **BELOW:** In addition to answering our clients' needs, and respecting Nouvel's architecture, the project made a third demand on our abilities: deferring to the views. In so doing, we sought to craft interiors that convey a subtly supportive power, a quietly noble environment from which to behold a majestic metropolis.

This project is unusual in that our work was confined entirely to interior decoration. Yet we were excited to take it on: the residence, in a building designed by Robert A. M. Stern and looking north across Central Park, required that we create a prototype—tasteful, modern, yet shot through with glamour—for the ultimate pied-à-terre in the sky. The entry hall features a stunning plasterwork finish, which reflects lights and views off of the ceiling and walls. **OPPOSITE:** The living room's furniture plan is oriented toward the park view, and the judiciously curated furnishings include a pair of Kàmptô armchairs and a Kevin Walz daybed from Pucci. The design makes a virtue of accumulated small details, such as the ruffled bands stitched into the curtains at the level of the window mullions.

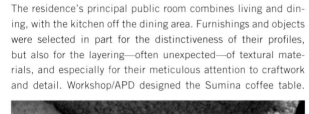

The residence's principal public room combines living and dining, with the kitchen off the dining area. Furnishings and objects were selected in part for the distinctiveness of their profiles, but also for the layering—often unexpected—of textural materials, and especially for their meticulous attention to craftwork and detail. Workshop/APD designed the Sumina coffee table.

OPPOSITE and BELOW: While it is not uncommon to rely on iconic design "brand names" when selecting objects for an interior, at our firm, luxury is spelled C-R-A-F-T. Most conspicuous, in this regard, in the dining area are the floating console, which was designed in-house, and the Noto chandelier by Brooklyn artisan Stephen Antonson. LEFT: We wrapped the media room in grass cloth, a material that delivers an elevated dose of reassuring retro charm. A pair of travertine nesting tables supports the cozy sectional sofa.

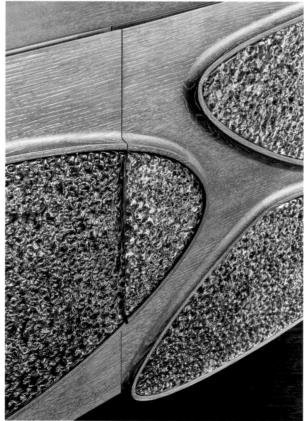

The Halabala armchair, Wilde bench, and Studio Van den Akker's Gerard pendant light accompany the Workshop/APD-designed bed and nightstands in a corner bedroom with a view that can best be described as humbling. Surely the apartment's most stunning design moment is the tableau behind the bed, constructed of overlapping leather panels and inspired by an image of Italian archways discovered in the course of our research. The sense of majestic, receding space in a classical context enables us to answer the incomparable urban view with style and substance.

Just south of the Jean Nouvel penthouse, our office created another loft pied-à-terre, with a similar Hudson River view, in a building by another architectural eminence, Richard Meier. Here we treated the center of the space as the dense core that held the program, while reserving the water-facing perimeter for open-plan living and dining. The kitchen, which connects the entry hall and the main room, illustrates the idea governing the core: we thought of it as a candy apple with a rich outer shell and crisp interior. The striking kitchen stools are by Avenue Road.

OPPOSITE and ABOVE: The architecture's extreme rectilinear character compelled us to introduce softer notes in the carpet and upholstery, and opposing geometries in the furnishings (such as the chandelier by John Procario), to serve as counterpoints to the building's elegant right-angled box. **FOLLOWING PAGES:** A custom smoked mirror installation proves that sometimes the best way to celebrate a view is to disrupt it.

If absolute privacy is not achievable (or, indeed, desirable), it is often the case that the illusion of it will psychologically suffice: thus the wall of floor-to-ceiling Corian shelves that lightly screens off the bedroom from the neighbors, directly across the street. Counterintuitively, given the loft's comparatively low ceiling height, we dropped the top of the sleeping nook, which gives it the snug, cozy character of a ship's cabin.

OUT OF MANY, ONE

For the first decade of Workshop/APD's existence, the two of us, for all intents and purposes, *were* the firm. We drew the plans and elevations, selected the materials and finishes, visited the furniture showrooms, interfaced with the contractors and their subs. Like most young firms (and many middle-aged ones), we did it all, and the fullness of our engagement proved deeply satisfying. When you're hungry, everything is felt more intensely, so that even a quiet day spent philosophizing, conceptualizing—spitballing—can be luminous.

Now we employ, on average, about eighty people, and have even welcomed a partner, Tom Zoli, who oversees all of the firm's architectural work with a felicitous blend of Andrew's swift conceptualizing skills and Matt's penchant for asking the right questions. Moreover, the second and third letters appended to the firm's name, representing the product and design disciplines, have ascended to the stature of architecture, which means that Workshop/APD provides services that are neither of our core competencies. We won't say that we've arrived. But the two guys who, once upon a time, sat across a card table doing everything now oversee a midsize dream factory, and have entered the complex, delicate space between creating and visioning.

That doesn't mean that our hands are not still firmly on the tiller, but rather that we convey our contributions differently. Everyone in the office understands that we love a reveal, that we take a great interest in the way materials come together, because we've told these stories so many times that our collaborators have internalized them—they don't need additional prompting to know the things we're predisposed to like. But it's no less the case that Workshop/APD remains a collective, rather than a top-down design firm, so we now serve, in many cases, as editors: not tasking or micromanaging but rather inspiring or questioning, making sure that multiple points of view have been considered, occasionally steering the conversation. When you know, as we do, that the people with whom you're entrusting projects are talented, committed, and have a genuine stake in the outcome, frankly, it's a bit of a relief. Not always having to initiate, watching others come up with inspired ideas, frees us to be creative in new ways—to think differently.

And that difference, to be sure, is potent. In certain quarters, there is the assumption—the suspicion—that if one goes to a "starchitect" for a project, the marquee name won't actually be the one who does the work. We won't say that, sometimes, this isn't the case. But it's more often true that constructing a great office is in its way as meaningful and lasting an achievement as authoring a great building. Being able to motivate, then coalesce,

different sensibilities—to create a cohesive, singular vision built out of a multitude of diverse perspectives—requires significant talent; indeed, one might say that it is talent's essence. We long ago ceased to be a two-man band. But designing an office to become the equal of those of our architectural heroes is every bit as exciting, challenging, and rewarding.

The business of life and the business of business run on their own motors, and though we're the leaders now, from time to time we struggle to stay in our lanes. It's a bit of a shame, that we can't still be twenty-three years old and getting our hands dirty—the firm's work has, to be sure, gotten better, but there's a nostalgia for those scrappy little projects that are, alas, receding in the rearview mirror.

And yet. Each of us has a moment in life when we feel that we've become precisely the person we hoped to be; the challenge is to keep that person fixed in time, while also allowing him or her to age gracefully. Call it the space between the youthful ideal and the inexorable march of Chronos. By building a firm, day by day, with individuals who manifest the vitality, enthusiasm, and optimism that was ours when we opened our doors, we—and, more to the point, the work that we do—can show the maturity of experience while remaining, we hope, forever young.

Though this Nantucket home had to conform in every particular to the island's strictly enforced aesthetic codes, it nonetheless represents tradition viewed through the lens of contemporary life. Arranged on two adjoining lots, the residence is comprised of three structures: a main building by the water, and two subordinate guest cottages, connected by a subterranean passageway and with a shared swimming pool and outdoor areas between them, at a higher elevation.

The main stair lies to the immediate right of the front door, in an arrangement combining a solid, upside-down sawtooth structure ascending from wood and marble plinths flanked by organic craftworks. The monolithic character of the stairway (as opposed to the typical openwork balusters) is surprising—and deliberate: it focuses the eye on what lies ahead, and subtly compels forward motion from the entry.

Upon entering, one finds a casual yet compelling, boho-chic living space with a conversation-stopping view of the harbor, which feels close enough to reach out and touch. A pair of folding glass panels opens fully to connect indoor and outdoor spaces.

In the spirit of relaxed beachcombing, we forsook a conventional hearth and instead installed an indoor version of an outdoor fire-pit. The furniture invites lounging, while the soaring shaped ceiling, finished in white oak, celebrates the room's relaxed character.

PREVIOUS PAGES: The custom-built banquette beneath the dining room windows encourages leisurely meals, and the wire-brushed shiplap boards suggest a room that was once an open space. Russell Pinch designed the Anders pendant lights, and the Entwine credenza is by Workshop/APD. **RIGHT and BELOW:** The multifunctional kitchen island is paired with Gervasoni chairs by Paola Navone.

OPPOSITE: This bath, in the primary suite, incorporates a feature that, to us, represents the acme of luxe: intercommunicating indoor and outdoor showers. The room's Davani stone trays and sinks, marble walls, and chevron-patterned floor were designed to give it hospitality flavor. **ABOVE:** Effectively in its own pavilion, the primary bedroom projects outward from the main volume of the house, enabling it to capture natural light on three sides.

Though at a distance from the harbor, the guest cottages, with their al fresco dining area, exposed fireplace, expansive decking, pool, planted beds, and—not least—long views, offer their own abundant charms, as well as privacy from the main house.

Animation derives from explosions of pattern and color, which contravene the sober traditionalism of the exterior and encourage a sense of fun. A relaxed open plan, poufs and decorative baskets, and a hanging fireplace straight out of 1960s Hollywood add to the mood.

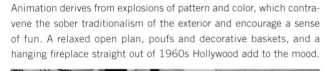

OPPOSITE: We exploited every opportunity to encourage wit and whimsy, at the micro scale as well as the macro. **ABOVE:** In a guesthouse powder room, we took the chevron pattern from the floor of the main house, colorized it, and applied it to the walls.

OPPOSITE: The underground tunnel running between the guest cottages enabled us to create a connection while keeping the space between the two buildings open, unobstructed, and functional. Area Environments wallpaper establishes an appropriately dramatic mood, and family photos set in glass frames keep things personal. **THIS PAGE:** The light at the end of the tunnel.

GOING GOING...

The American artist Fred Sandback (1943–2003) isn't a household name. But his work, and perhaps especially if you're an architect, is uncanny. Sandback remains best known for his "yarn sculptures," which he created by stretching acrylic yarn into perfectly formed, outsized geometric shapes—triangles, rectangles, and the like—and positioning them in otherwise empty galleries. In so doing, and with the absolute bare minimum of material, the lightest of interventions, Sandback conveyed a powerful sense of spatial presence: drawing lines in the air, as it were, the artist trusted that our perceptual instincts would do the rest, and he was right—in our minds we see divisions, we make rooms, and, not least, we grasp the metaphysical nature of reality. Sandback's oeuvre is the acme of simplicity. Yet its impact is as haunting, as profound, as Richard Serra's monumental waves of steel.

Mies van der Rohe famously spoke of his desire to reduce architecture to "almost nothing"—yet as Sandback's work (and, for that matter, Mies's buildings) demonstrate, it takes a whole lot of "something" to make "nothing" into a success. The trap, ironically, is that if you belabor the idea of nothingness, you end up with a something that feels forced, contrived, or overthought. Aware of this, we strive to make architecture that feels natural and inevitable, and doesn't require a master's degree to be understood or enjoyed: architecture that just *is*. We've talked at length, in these pages, about "the spaces between" various opposing aspects of our craft. But there is none trickier to traverse than the space between doing too little and doing too much.

There are many ways to go about striking a balance, of course, but two examples suggest how it can be managed. The first we might describe as being consciously mindful of the issue's complexities, as was the case in a full-floor loft apartment we designed on Manhattan's far west side *(p. 182)*. The space itself was spectacular:

the top floor, 360-degree views, 14-foot-high ceilings. What's more, the building's design, by the French architect Jean Nouvel, featured a skin comprised largely of a multitude of different size glass panels, each tilted inward or outward to varying degrees. From without, this creates the effect of a gigantic faceted jewel perched beside the Hudson River; from within, the undulating windows give the views a prismatic, undeniably vitalizing character.

Our clients, dedicated collectors of contemporary art, wanted the apartment to serve as a private gallery of sorts, and to foreground the world beyond the windows. Unfortunately—as in many such buildings, the original floor plan was an afterthought—the assumption being that whoever bought the place would immediately gut it and start over.

Which is what we did. But before reprogramming the space, we applied the mindfulness principle and asked ourselves, What, truly, are we being called upon to do? The answer, unmistakably, was: As little as possible. So we moved the living areas away from the perimeter, crafted white-lacquered millwork walls that replicated the undulating language of the windows, and simplified the details to capture the character of a gallery. The outcome creates a sublime condition defined by ever-changing natural light, entrancing views, and lightly zoned spaces in which the architecture makes very little impression—and all the difference. It took a lot of forethought and consideration—a lot of "something." But in the end, we managed to disappear in just the right way.

The other example represents precisely the opposite, a classic instance of not judging, not overthinking, and above all not bringing too much "mind" to the drafting table. For this Shingle-Style residence in the Hamptons *(p. 278)*, Andrew took the lead, and for the first time in his twenty-five-year career, he didn't visit the project prior to designing, but rather empowered the team to be on-site while he worked from plans, elevations and images, and served as editor. A vision evolved very quickly. We didn't second-guess it, we executed the work with rigor, consistency, and commitment, and the whole thing got done in under eight months.

And when we saw the photographs, none of us could believe it—we were all stunned. The house has the beauty, simplicity, and serenity of a chapel: it is one of the finest projects the office has ever produced. We cannot say we expected it—in our minds, we were responding to a set of circumstances and trusting ourselves and one another. And that response transformed into something of which we are all immensely proud.

Of course, one of the most difficult decisions in any creative endeavor is determining when it's done, and every artist strives to find a working method that delivers the decisive moment in a way that feels artless. Fred Astaire, it is said, would practice every step of every routine dozens of times—and then, when it came time to perform, he'd throw it all away and just *dance*. Others devote lifetimes to the elimination of the unnecessary, a quest that occasioned an oft-quoted observation from Frédéric Chopin. "After one has played a vast quantity of notes and more notes," said the maestro, "it is simplicity that emerges as the crowning reward of art."

To us, it is an entirely familiar journey. After a quarter century of practice, Workshop/APD continues to refine our own working method, one that brings us to a point of conclusion, on every project, that seems as if it could have gone no other way. In the spaces between a thing and its opposite, a dream and a reality, between Matt's desire to hang on and Andrew's wish to let go, lies the perfect conclusion. Where we will find it tomorrow, we can't say. But for now—we're done.

Residential modernism can prove difficult to design, as the style cues are instinctual: they involve things like massing, scale, proportion, and flow as opposed to details like shingles or pilasters. When we were engaged to create this residence in Stuart, Florida, we challenged ourselves to reach for some timeless architectural virtues: purity, simplicity, and lucidity. Entering from the motor court, one discovers a zone designed to mediate between realms both public and private, exterior and interior: a forecourt, with a sculptural piece "floating" in a reflecting pool, offering a glimpse of what is to come through a soaring, double-height window wall exposing the grand staircase.

Just as the forecourt bridges two worlds, so too does the house's living room, which looks back to the human-made environment of the entry and *its* water feature, and forward to nature and its water feature—in this case, the Atlantic Ocean. The black granite benches were designed to serve as both seating and sculpture: their waveform surfaces suggest the water's undulations.

The treads of the floating stair are constructed from the house's predominating material: travertine marble, found as well in the floors and baths within, and the decks and stairs outside. Fourteen-foot-high windows in the dining room draw the house's swimming pool into the living experience. Scale and intimacy derive from the "flying buttress" element above the water, which casts the pool as an outdoor room.

PREVIOUS PAGES, ABOVE, and OPPOSITE: The temple-like rigor of the waterside elevation (which owes much, we confess, to Mies van der Rohe), the strongly horizontal character of the design, at once embraces the linear character of the waterline and landscape and contrasts with the rough, haphazard condition of the beach.

This triplex can be found on one of the most elegant residential blocks on Manhattan's Upper West Side, and enjoys iconic views. Yet owing to eccentricities both spatial and architectural, we chose to embrace what might be described as haute whimsy rather than straitlaced tradition. The outcome features three conditions: one reflecting the district's historic character, another given to the joys of penthouse living, and a third devoted to play. **OPPOSITE and ABOVE:** The slatted two-story wall in the entry, at the foot of the main stair, is backed by a mirror panel, which adds depth and captures and reflects light. The vertical ribbing becomes translucent on the second floor, and gives way entirely to a glass window that frames a view of the children's study area at the top of the stairs.

The walls in the double-height living room are finished in a decorative plaster, which reinforces the residence's sense of history. A Workshop/APD-designed double-sided sofa in the room's center lends scale to the grand circumstances, and anchors an elegant modern design scheme featuring Wabi chairs, a sofa and side tables from Avenue Road, and David Weeks's Mobile chandelier.

The kitchen/dining/family room, on the apartment's second floor, tells a distinctly different story from the more formal living room below, and in a more contemporary language that mixes wood, metal, and stone. A vintage crystal console dances with light and color, while the vertical ribbing on the millwork wall finds echoes in the lines of the sofa and the wood-clad club chairs.

The primary suite is located on the residence's first floor, as are the children's bedrooms. There is a material richness to the space, which embraces the decorative plaster walls, the Workshop/APD-designed leather headboard and bed, and Eskayel's voluptuous custom Cyrrus carpet, which is illuminated by the abundant southern light.

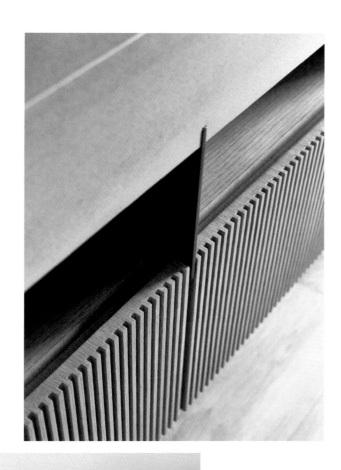

Vintage buildings often come with age-related challenges—but more often they offer singular, even stunning opportunities. In this instance, we were able to annex one of the structure's turrets and transform it into a playroom for the kids, an incomparable aerie with a ceiling height of nearly twenty-five feet. Very few children, it must be admitted, ever get to experience so rarefied a treehouse—let alone one with a dramatic double climbing wall and professional belay system.

Often architects are engaged to remove preexisting detail and replace it with clean, minimal raw space that embraces the pleasures of loft living. Here, in one of the most exquisitely beautiful of the cast-iron former industrial buildings in New York's historic SoHo district, our firm was invited to do precisely the opposite: to take an open-plan loft devoid of any aesthetic embellishment and transform it, with casework, mouldings, materials, and finishes, into an apartment that would have been at home in prewar Paris. **OPPOSITE and THIS PAGE:** In the newly conceived vestibule, we extended the terrazzo floor upward to frame a Deco-inspired entry console, with smoked mirrors that reflect the front door and a bronze drawer set into the stepped stone.

OPPOSITE, ABOVE, and FOLLOWING PAGES: The open kitchen, set between the entry and the main living room, faces a sitting area elegantly constructed by our client, himself an interior designer. To make the zone suitable for both food preparation and entertaining, we created millwork panels that can conceal the kitchen's functional elements and make it feel more akin to the bar in a stylish hotel's cocktail lounge.

OPPOSITE, THIS PAGE, and FOLLOWING PAGES: The long main room—which runs nearly the full width of the residence—faces east and enjoys large glazed doors and transom windows from end to end. So that the owners could take full advantage of the light, air, and views, we took the unusual step of setting the primary suite directly behind the living room, separating the public and private realms with a full-height, partially mirrored bar and display cabinet. In this respect, despite our "historic" mouldings and coffered ceilings, the apartment still retains the character of a classic loft—as we prefer to think of it, the best of both worlds.

This part of Brooklyn is classified as a historic district, but this particular block is not landmarked—an important distinction, as it enabled us to insert a new single-family townhouse, the design of which remained entirely unrestricted. Though the style is contemporary, we selected a handmade Belgian brick, long and narrow, as a primary façade material, which suits the larger historical context.

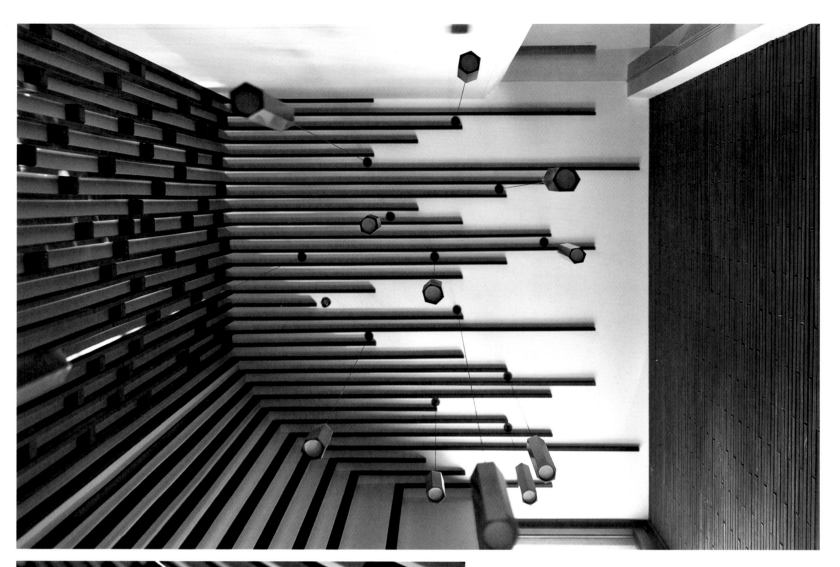

The Belgian brick continues into the entry vestibule, a compressed space that rises up three stories to form a highly theatrical atrium. As a firm, we often use screen elements as dividers, and also to introduce depth, texture, and materiality (and to filter daylight). Here the banded and fluted elements that form the screen ascend dramatically, then cross the ceiling and support an array of hanging lights suspended at different heights above the vestibule.

PREVIOUS PAGES: To the right of the entry, separated by the three-story screen wall, is the dining room, which overlooks the street. **RIGHT and BELOW:** The kitchen is directly behind the dining room (it can be glimpsed through the double-sided wine cooler), and as it is the heart of the home for this culinary-minded family, we took pains to give it a special distinction, with millwork panels that separate it stylistically from the living and dining areas. **FOLLOWING PAGES:** The living room sits directly behind the kitchen and is effectively an extension of it. The glass door to the left of the expansive bookcase provides access to the rear garden.

The primary suite occupies the entirety of the second floor, with a private deck off of the bedroom. This level of the house was stepped back to enable the addition of a generous private terrace overlooking the garden.

Like the circulation spine on the main floor directly below, the primary suite's axis extends from the bedroom at the rear of the house into the bath, with its capacious wet room, in front. The Pietra Cardosa stone is repeated throughout the house.

The translucent floor-to-ceiling bathroom window faces the street and fills the long, narrow space with daylight. In this instance, as with many of our infill projects, the objective is to pull natural illumination as deep into the interior as possible.

OPPOSITE: While the street-facing façade is largely opaque, the five-story townhouse's rear elevation remains almost fully glazed. LEFT: Off the lower-level family room, an outdoor sitting area forms an adjunct to the larger rear garden. An outdoor kitchen sits beneath the stairs that descend from the living room. BELOW: A brushed stainless-steel hot tub on the rooftop terrace offers sweeping 360-degree views.

Engaged to completely reimagine the interiors in this traditional post-and-beam Hamptons residence, we set off what might be characterized as a gentle architectural explosion: creating a cathedral-like double-height space by removing the floor at the building's center, replacing solids with vertical slats, and dipping the entirety in cream—opening the spaces to one another vertically and horizontally, and filling the home with a serene, pure glow.

The family room incorporates similar pieces, differently deployed and with a slightly different color palette: the Perriand stool reappears, as do jute area rugs, from Stark, which are used throughout the home. They are joined by armchairs in the style of Pierre Jeanneret, a Balsamo coffee table in travertine, and a burl wood side table, all of which subtly disrupt the sea of white.

The dining room shifts the narrative again, with distinctively shaped dining chairs from Artemest in a yet lighter shade of wood around a custom table, all beneath an utterly minimal T2 chandelier in black-finished brass.

The kitchen is, if anything, even whiter but takes color and form from the garden views, and from the Shaker-style Inmod beech counter stools with cream-colored leather seat cushions. What we discovered is that committing to an exceptionally rigorous design idea can enable a truly distinctive outcome with the simplest of building blocks.

Our office designed the custom upholstered bed in the primary suite. Continuing the craft motif, the nightstand lamps are hand-carved stone; the graceful pendant is from Fontana Arte. In the primary bath, the organic lounge chair from Jayson Home appears to be made of stone but is in fact a light, durable resin.

EPILOGUE

ENORMOUS CHANGES AT THE LAST MINUTE

"We're done"—or so we thought.

It would be incorrect to say that everything you've just read is inaccurate or irrelevant—quite the contrary. We stand by it all. But just as a mere four-degree destabilization transformed the campanile in Pisa from a handsome fourteenth-century Romanesque building into an object entirely, unrepeatably unique, so too has a seismic shift in the global condition left Workshop/APD (in the poet's words) changed, changed utterly.

It would be hard, as we all know too well, to overstate the impact of the first global pandemic in a century on the collective human psyche. For the world's citizens, wrenched from normality by a trauma without end, nothing will ever be the same. Surely not for us, who both got sick and thankfully recovered. More to the point: In the face of the collapse of one's everyday assumptions, the extraneous falls away, leaving a silence in which nothing remains but the essential; truly, we discover what we're made of. And what the experience of struggling with ourselves, one another, our collaborators, our clients, and our work under the yoke of COVID has revealed is that the spaces between—all of them—are richer than either of us, despite twenty-five years in business and even longer as friends, could possibly have imagined.

How has Andrew changed? In a way, like all of us have: the recognition of life's evanescence has infused him with a new benignity—his "what is" is more expansive, less deterministic. At work, this has led Andrew to the realization that success comes more readily, dependably, from encouragement than a critical perspective, and he's revealed himself to be a leader of sensitivity and vision. Andrew's constructive support and consoling stability have helped to navigate Workshop/APD through a troubled, uncertain time.

What happened to Matt? He responded to Andrew's openness, the ebb of critique, by becoming less guarded and more communicative, a bottomless sharer of ideas, information, and inspiration. It's not that Matt has stopped asking "what if?"—rather, he is able to deploy his Socratic approach in a more profligate fashion, applying his unexpectedly broad bandwidth to multiple simultaneous projects with unflagging interest and enthusiasm, and without fear of censure.

With the release, under the moment's duress, of habits and attitudes that, in truth, we weren't even aware of, each of us has observed the other's strengths come out in unique ways, and so much of what we value in one another has been elevated. We see each other—and, consequently, the work—differently, and in so doing we have rebuilt the foundational structure of a great creative partnership and, to borrow a phrase, a beautiful friendship. Remarkably, in the past, the two of us consulted only occasionally. Now, we seek each other's wisdom on a daily basis, and offer and receive ideas, paradigms, confidences with joy as opposed to judgment. COVID remains an unspeakable scourge, an epic tragedy. Yet we're grateful that, confronted with it, we didn't turn on one another: the moment, horrible as it is, brought out our best.

And not just *our* best. At Workshop/APD, a core group of half a dozen individuals has, for some fifteen years, engaged with us in an osmotic exercise: in which our sensibilities have seeped into their understanding of the firm's philosophy and style, and our design vision has in some measure been driven by our awareness of what this exceptional team can do. In the past year, we've come to recognize that this is not a hierarchy but rather a true and fruitful creative collaboration—even as our colleagues have embraced our newly rejuvenated spirit of encouragement and openness. Accordingly, these individuals, especially under the present circum-

stances, have increasingly stepped up and shown an eagerness to execute their own visions—to lead. As well, we have increasingly seen Tom Zoli, our third partner, step into the space that once was a duologue—to go from being Workshop/APD's not-so-secret secret weapon to being a genuine, profoundly influential coequal.

As a result, even as our office has become abuzz with new clients—the urge to nest having energized exponentially as the necessity of nesting has skyrocketed—our work has become more assured, more unified at every scale, more comprehensive, and more inspired visually, programmatically, and in relation to the larger world—in every sense, more complete. You might say that the space between the beauty that lived in our minds' eyes and our ability to transform those fantasies into built reality—*that* space has grown ever more bridgeable. The office-wide ability to breathe, to listen and to hear, indeed to dream, has taken Workshop/APD to a better, more mature state of being.

So—yes. There is our history prior to the onset of the pandemic, when we saw the world one way, and the entirely unanticipated transit that has led us to another point of view—but not, by any means, a conclusion. Workshop/APD resides, at the present moment, in the tantalizing, slightly terrifying space between yesterday and tomorrow. Uncertain yet exhilarated, we are above all deeply moved, to have been afforded the chance to learn, to contemplate where we're going through the prism of where we've been: a space filled with gratitude, not so much for what the firm has accomplished, but the many gifts that we as individuals have been given. As another old song goes, "the future's not ours to see"—but, in all humility, Workshop/APD remains better prepared for whatever is to come than it has ever been.

Now we're done…for now.

PHOTOGRAPHY CREDITS / PROJECT INFORMATION

THE COURTYARD HOUSE
Nantucket, MA / Photographed by Read McKendree / Workshop/APD Project Team: Bronsin Ablon, Nickie Anderson, Tyler Chavers, Dirk De Beer, Michael Ellison, Naz Ertugrul, Zoe Gavil, Andrew Kline, Daisy Lan, Jongseok Lee, Michael Luft-Weissberg, Elena Rizzi, Tarika Thienapirak, Ruoxi Wang, Thomas J. Zoli / Collaborators: Reid Builders, Craft Engineering Studio, Ahern LLC Landscape Architecture

CENTRAL PARK DUPLEX
New York, NY / Photographed by Read McKendree and Amanda James / Workshop/APD Project Team: Tyler Chavers, Adam Dello Buono, Michael Ellison, Felix Guzman, Daisy Lan, Brook Quach, Stephan Thimme, Constantina Tsiara, Ruoxi Wang, Court Whisman, Thomas J. Zoli / Collaborators: Highline Construction, Craft Engineering Studio, CES, EENY A/V, Rare Culture Art Advisory, Union Digital Art Advisory

COLLECTOR'S RETREAT
New York, NY / Photographed by Donna Dotan / Workshop/APD Project Team: Juan Francisco Brown, Dan Burns, Michael Ellison, Hines Fischer, Felix Guzman, Natalie Kamei, Brook Quach, Sacha Roubeni, Stephan Thimme, Christina Thompson, Ellen Yersavich, Ruoxi Wang / Collaborators: Helen Crowther, SilverLining Interiors, Inc., RHL Engineering

WESTCHESTER VIEWS
Armonk, NY / Photographed by Read McKendree / Workshop/APD Project Team: Nickie Anderson, Tyler Chavers, Michael Ellison, Naz Ertugrul, Andy Hart, Andrew Kline, Daisy Lan, Tarika Thienapirak, Thomas J. Zoli / Collaborators: ABC Construction, Craft Engineering Studio, Frank Guiliano

MUSEUM MILE DUPLEX
New York, NY / Photographed by Donna Dotan / Workshop/APD Project Team: Zachary Helmers, J. Tyler Marshall, Sacha Roubeni / Collaborators: JGSK Design, Unlimited Designs, Craft Engineering Studio, Caliper Studio

BAHAMAS PRIVATE RESORT
Nassau, The Bahamas / Photographed by Read McKendree / Workshop/APD Project Team: Colin Campbell, Tyler Chavers, Danielle Davis, Michael Ellison, Hines Fischer, Kelsey Hutchins, Andrew Kline, Brian Thomas, Thomas J. Zoli / Collaborators: Capstone Homes, Murakami Design, Holbrook & Associates Landscape Architects

WACCABUC LAKE HOUSE
Waccabuc, NY / Photographed by Donna Dotan / Workshop/APD Project Team: Kristyn Bock, Dan Burns, Andy Hart, Natalie Kamei, Jubilee Kang, Brook Quach, Stephan Thimme, Christina Thompson / Collaborators: ABC Construction, Murray Engineering Studio, GFX Site Development, Gunn Landscape Architecture

WEST VILLAGE DUPLEX
New York, NY / Photographed by Donna Dotan / Workshop/APD Project Team: Dan Burns, Carlos Canella, Zachary Helmers, Natalie Kamei, J. Tyler Marshall, Kaitlin McQuaide, Thomas J. Zoli / Collaborators: Foundations Interior Design Group, Craft Engineering, Argosy Designs

ASPEN SKI RETREAT
Aspen, CO / Photographed by Read McKendree and Rob Millman / Workshop/APD Project Team: Dan Burns, Michael Ellison, Hines Fischer, Zachary Helmers, Natalie Kamei, Jubilee Kang, J. Tyler Marshall, Christina Thompson / Collaborators: Brikor Associates, Connect One Design, Poss Architecture + Planning

PALM BEACH MODERN
Palm Beach, FL / Photographed by Read McKendree / Workshop/APD Project Team: Tyler Chavers, Michael Ellison, Zachary Helmers, Daisy Lan, Angela Lee, Michelle Zar / Collaborators: Smith & Moore Architects, Seabreeze Building

PEBBLE BEACH ESCAPE
Pebble Beach, CA / Photographed by Read McKendree / Workshop/APD Project Team: Tyler Chavers, Michael Ellison, Felix Guzman, Faith Hoops, Andrew Kline, Selin Kurun, Daisy Lan, Irina Matos, Jason Money, Rodrigo Zamora, Thomas J. Zoli / Collaborators: Andrew Lino Construction

HUDSON RIVER PENTHOUSE
New York, NY / Photographed by Donna Dotan / Workshop/APD Project Team: Dan Burns, Tyler Chavers, Natalie Kamei, Jubilee Kang, Brook Quach, Stephan Thimme, Christina Thompson / Collaborators: S. Donadic, Inc., D'Antonio Consulting Engineers, Gunn Landscape Architecture

ELEVATED AERIE
New York, NY / Photographed by Read McKendree / Workshop/APD Project Team: Bronsin Ablon, Michael Ellison, Nicole Ficano, Ruoxi Wang / Collaborators: Artspace

PERRY STREET PIED-A-TERRE
New York, NY / Photographed by Donna Dotan / Workshop/APD Project Team: Bronsin Ablon, Michael Ellison, Natalie Kamei, Angela Lee, Kaitlin McQuaide, Brook Quach, Sacha Roubeni, Stephan Thimme, Christina Thompson, Ruoxi Wang, Ellen Yersavich, Michelle Zar, Thomas J. Zoli / Collaborators: Mentors Construction, Inc.

NANTUCKET FAMILY COMPOUND
Nantucket, MA / Photographed by Read McKendree / Workshop/APD Project Team: Tyler Chavers, Hines Fischer, Andy Hart, Zachary Helmers, Kelsey Hutchins, Andrew Kline, Michael Luft-Weissberg, Irina Matos, Wesley Parietti, Tarika Thienapirak, Ellen Yersavich, Michelle Zar, Thomas J. Zoli / Collaborators: Reid Builders, Craft Engineering Studio, Concentric Fabrication, Ahern LLC Landscape Design

STUART FLORIDA HOUSE
Stuart, FL / Photographed by Read McKendree and Amanda James / Workshop/APD Project Team: Colin Campbell, Michael Ellison, Nicole Ficano, Andy Hart, Andrew Kline, Michael Luft-Weissberg, Tarika Thienapirak, Brian Thomas, Scott Topel, Ruoxi Wang / Collaborators: First Florida Development & Construction, Inc., Craft Engineering Studio, CES, Howard F. Ostrout Jr. & Assoc. Landscape Architecture

UPPER WEST SIDE TRIPLEX
New York, NY / Photographed by Donna Dotan / Workshop/APD Project Team: Nickie Anderson, Tyler Chavers, Michael Ellison, Tommy Harris, Daisy Lan, Colin Murtaugh, Brook Quach, Atique Rahman, Elena Rizzi, Sacha Roubeni, Stephan Thimme, Ruoxi Wang, Thomas J. Zoli / Collaborators: Highline Construction, Craft Engineering Studio, CES

CLASSIC CONTEMPORARY APARTMENT
New York, NY / Photographed by Adrian Gaut / Workshop/APD Project Team: Adam Dello Buono, Olivia Manzano, Amanda March, Brook Quach, Stephan Thimme, Thomas J. Zoli / Collaborators: Studio Todd Raymond, Mentors Construction, Inc.

COBBLE HILL TOWNHOUSE
Brooklyn, NY / Photographed by Donna Dotan and Shannon Dupre / Workshop/APD Project Team: Juan Francisco Brown, Andy Hart, Zachary Helmers, James Krapp, J. Tyler Marshall, Thomas J. Zoli / Collaborators: April Bovet Interior Design, R. Sutton & Co, Craft Engineering Studio, Gunn Landscape Architecture

HAMPTONS MINIMALISM
Sagaponack, NY / Photographed by Read McKendree / Workshop/APD Project Team: Colin Campbell, Tyler Chavers, Michael Ellison, Daisy Lan, Angela Lee, Jason Money, Michelle Zar, Thomas J. Zoli / Nocera General Contracting, Barbara Cartategui Art Advisory

ESSAY REFERENCES

DIAGRAMMING PROGRAM
New York, NY / Photographed by Eric Laignel / Referenced on page 15, *A State of Becoming*

FLUID ZONES
New York, NY / Photographed by Donna Dotan / Referenced on page 15, *A State of Becoming*

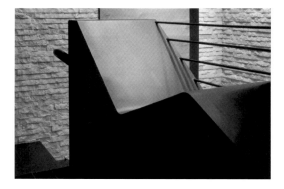

MODERN MATERIALITY
New York, NY / Photographed by Tom Olcott / Referenced on page 15, *A State of Becoming*

HISTORIC JEWEL BOX
New York, NY / Photographed by Tom Olcott / Referenced on page 59, *The Joy of Letting Go*

NAVIGATING SPACE
Nantucket, MA / Photographed by Yellow Productions / Referenced on page 58, *The Joy of Letting Go*

CRAFT, TEXTURE & MATERIAL
New York, NY / Photographed by Tom Olcott / Referenced on page 98, *Hand,* and opposite

TRIBECA LOFT
New York, NY / Photographed by Tom Olcott / Referenced on page 98, *Hand*

BROOKLYN NAVY YARD BLDG 92
Brooklyn, NY / Photographed by Chuck Choi / Referenced on page 132, *History—Past and Present*

TUDOR ESTATE
Greenwich, CT / Photographed by Read McKendree / Referenced on page 133, *History—Past and Present*

ACKNOWLEDGMENTS

Through this book, we set out to offer a view of our journey as friends, professionals, and designers. Over the course of our careers we have learned that the best projects come from the most passionate collaborations, and our book is certainly an example of that mission.

This process has been illuminating, forcing us to look within and reflect on our journey along the way. We are so grateful to all the people who have helped bring the project to life, in particular Charles Miers, Ron Broadhurst, Maria-Pia Gramaglia, and Alyn Evans at Rizzoli, who encouraged us to show our work to the world and guided us steadily along the way, and to Jill Cohen and Melissa Powell who have navigated this ship through truly unprecedented waters. Thank you to Marc Kristal, the literary genius who took our ramblings and turned them into a coherent (and fun) story; Sam Shahid and Matthew Kraus, our brilliant graphic designers, who held firm to their convictions and presented our work so beautifully; our gifted photographers, Donna Dotan and Read McKendree, who imbue new meaning through their lenses; and our tireless in-house marketing team, Lisa Jasper and David McEachin, who somehow juggled the Herculean task of managing this project from inception to completion along with everything else they do.

We want to thank the amazing team of people, past and present, who we have had the privilege of working with over the past twenty-two years. Words cannot express the gratitude we feel for the exceptionally talented architects, designers, project managers, and support staff, and the coaches, consultants, craftspeople, builders, artists, and suppliers without whom the work would not be possible. Most importantly, a deep thank you to our partner, Tom Zoli, who grounds us, challenges us, and brings an acute architectural eye to everything he does. We were also fortunate to be inspired by great educators and mentors, especially Tony Viscardi, who helped us tap into our creative instincts and pushed us to question everything we see.

Last, but certainly not least, thank you to our families—our parents and siblings who encouraged us, our spouses who put up with us, our children who inspire us, and our pets who calm us—this journey would not have been possible without your support and love.

First published in the United States of America in 2022 by
Rizzoli International Publications, Inc.
300 Park Avenue South
New York, NY 10010
www.rizzoliusa.com

Copyright © 2022 by Workshop/APD

Designed by Sam Shahid and Matthew Kraus

Photograph page 300 by Lesley Unruh

Publisher: Charles Miers
Editor: Ron Broadhurst
Managing Editor: Lynn Scrabis
Production Manager: Alyn Evans

Developed in collaboration with Jill Cohen Associates, LLC

Printed and bound in Italy

2022 2023 2024 2025 2026 / 10 9 8 7 6 5 4 3 2 1

ISBN: 978-0-8478-7248-0
Library of Congress Control Number: 2022935672

Visit us online:
Facebook.com/RizzoliNewYork
Twitter: @Rizzoli_Books
Instagram.com/RizzoliBooks
Pinterest.com/RizzoliBooks
Youtube.com/user/RizzoliNY
Issuu.com/Rizzoli